FIRST EDITION

Alaska Cooking Classics

A Treasury of
Lodge and Bed & Breakfast
Favorite Recipes

Edited By
Mary Gerken & Cass Crandall

Illustrated By
Diana Tillion

KACHEMAK PUBLISHING • HOMER, ALASKA

PRINTED AND BOUND IN THE UNITED STATES OF AMERICA

ISBN 0-9626071-3-4

ISSN 1053-4989

LIBRARY OF CONGRESS CATALOG CARD NUMBER: 91-75068

PUBLISHED BY:

KACHEMAK PUBLISHING
P.O. BOX 470
HOMER, AK 99603

DESIGN BY:

KATHY DOOGAN

EDITORIAL ASSISTANCE:

L.J. CAMPBELL

COVER BY:

STEPHANIE LaFLEUR / LaFLEUR PRINTING & DESIGN

Contents

Foreword

Over the past several years, many delicious-sounding recipes have crossed my desk, sent in by the cooks and operators of lodges, inns and bed and breakfast establishments throughout Alaska. Unfortunately, all too often these recipes had to be dropped from our books, *Bed and Breakfast, Alaska Style!* and *Alaska Wilderness Lodges*, simply because there was not enough space. There are so many fine cooks and so many wonderful Alaskan recipes from our cities and out in "bush Alaska" that deserve appreciation that we decided to publish our first cookbook. Hence, *Alaska Cooking Classics!*

All of the recipes contained in this book were sent in by lodge, inn or B & B hosts and hostesses who have tested them on some of the most sophisticated, well-traveled palates in the world — Alaskan tourists. Included are many old Alaska favorites, from salmon to sourdough and everything in between, plus many secret recipes never shared before.

Mary Gerken, co-editor of *Alaska Cooking Classics*, owns and operates a fly-in fishing lodge on Lake Iliamna with her husband, Ted. Her years of experience as "chief cook and bottle-washer" at their remote lodge was invaluable when putting together this cookbook. Who knows better than Mary the special trials, tribulations and infinite rewards connected with serving an elite and hungry group of fishermen a gourmet meal in bush Alaska? In fact, life at their lodge is so unique, Ted wrote a book about it! Look for *Gamble At Iliamna* by Ted Gerken at your favorite bookstore, or write to Ted at Iliaska Lodge (address on page 235) for information on how you can get a copy.

—CASS CRANDALL

Introduction

A laskans have developed a unique style of cooking through the years, combining many styles brought here by explorers and pioneers. The Natives of Alaska also have their own specialties which have been adapted over the two centuries since the Russians brought their ways of cooking to the North.

In the 1800s Americans started fishing off Alaska and eventually settled here after the U.S. purchased the territory in 1867. The diversity of these settlers' ethnic backgrounds, plus an influx of Scandinavians in the late 1800s, strongly influenced Alaskan cooking. As the different cultures blended and cooks made do with what they had, a very distinctive food culture emerged.

Today, Alaskan cooks are blessed with an abundance of resources. Bounty from the sea includes many different fish, shellfish, mollusks and sea kelp. The land around us offers wild game, wild vegetables and wild berries and bountiful gardens flourish through the long summer days.

By the 1950s, Alaska's population had grown large enough to support regular produce shipments. I remember receiving apples and oranges for Christmas on the Alaska Steamship line at the newly built dock in Homer, realizing how very special they were. Some stores carried them regularly, but the cost was prohibitive. As a result, many people grew their own vegetables. Now many Alaskans keep gardens not just for the satisfaction, but because of the nutritional value and to have organically grown food.

Alaskans grow cabbages which exceed 50 pounds yet are still crisp and juicy. We also grow jumbo potatoes and the best crunchy turnips you've ever eaten. Cool temperatures and long days of the summer growing season make for great peas, crisp lettuce and top-notch broccoli and cauliflower. This rich harvest, in the hands of Alaska's creative cooks, has made for some great recipes.

As you will see when browsing through this book, it contains some of the very best we have to offer. Alaska's lodges are renowned for their ample portions of good food. And the state's bed and breakfast establishments are quickly gaining reputations for their hospitality and fine food.

Alaskan cooks like living off the land, using ingredients indigenous to their area, but it's also wonderful to have all the fruits and vegetables of the world available at our fingertips. Fresh produce is flown daily to supermarkets in Fairbanks, Anchorage and Juneau. Many remote areas are served by air carrier from these main hubs and receive grocery orders regularly. We have all learned the necessity of substitution though, and this has become the basis of many wonderful new recipes.

On the following pages, you'll find a lot of enticing breakfast entrees from successful bed and breakfast homes. There are quite a few fish recipes from the lodges, because that is what they do so well. There are also many other great recipes in many different categories which we invite you to try.

—MARY GERKEN

CHAPTER 1

While Waiting for the Fish to Bite

SNACKS, DIPS & SPREADS

BAKED CHEESE TWISTS

1 lb. Cheddar cheese, grated

3/4 C. soft butter

1 3/4 C. flour

1/2 t. cayenne pepper

1/2 t. salt

Preheat oven to 400 degrees. Beat cheese and butter together; add flour and spices (mixture will be like pie dough). Roll out on floured board until 1/4 inch thick. Cut into strips 1/2 inch x 4 inches. Hold ends of strip and twist a few times, then place on cookie sheet (ungreased) about 1 inch apart. Bake about 6 minutes until golden brown. Remove from sheets and cool. Variation: try Monterey jack cheese, jack and blue cheeses or jack cheese with caraway seeds.

— **TIMBERLINGS B & B,**
PALMER

CHEESE APPETIZERS

2 C. sharp Cheddar cheese, grated

1 C. margarine

2 C. self-rising flour

dash of salt

1/2 t. cayenne

2 C. Rice Krispies

Cream cheese and margarine well. Stir in flour, salt, cayenne and Rice Krispies. Drop by teaspoon on ungreased cookie sheet. Bake at 375 degrees for 10 minutes.

— **WINDSOCK INN,**
DOUGLAS

ALSATIAN ONION TART

pastry for 10-inch, 1-crust pie

1 egg beaten with 1 T. water

1 1/2 lbs. onions, peeled and
   thickly sliced

1/4 C. white wine (optional)

1/2 t. thyme

1 t. basil

1/2 t. salt

1 t. freshly ground black pepper

2 T. butter

1 t. olive oil

4 oz. ham or bacon, diced

2 eggs

1/2 C. whipping cream

3/4 lb. Swiss cheese, grated

parsley sprigs, for garnish

Roll out pastry and line a 10-inch tart pan with a removable bottom. Prick the base of the pastry with a fork, line with a circle of foil or parchment, then cover with baking beans. Bake at 350 degrees for 10 minutes, then remove lining and beans. Brush a little egg wash over crust and return to oven for 2 minutes. Repeat twice more.

For filling, put the onions in a saucepan with the wine, herbs, seasonings and butter. Cover and saute gently for about 10 minutes. Remove lid and let juices reduce completely.

Meanwhile, heat olive oil in a skillet and saute the ham or bacon until golden brown. Drain on paper towels.

When onion mixture and the pastry base are ready, mix the eggs and cream in a bowl. Gently stir in the onions and ham or bacon. Pour into the pastry base, spreading evenly. Top with the grated cheese and bake for 20 to 30 minutes until golden brown on top.

Transfer the pan to a cooling rack, removing the base and sides, and cool 5 to 10 minutes before serving. Garnish with parsley. Serves 10 as an appetizer, 6 as a main course.

— **GLACIER BAY COUNTRY INN,
GUSTAVUS**

HAM AND CHEESE APPETIZER CREPES

16 7- or 8-inch basic crepes

1 medium-sized onion, minced

2 T. butter

1 C. cooked ham, minced

1 large ripe tomato, peeled,
  seeded and chopped

1/2 t. leaf basil, crumbled

1/4 t. fennel seed, crushed

1/8 t. pepper

2 T. parsley, chopped

1 C. (4 oz.) Swiss cheese,
  shredded

1/4 C. butter, melted

1/2 C. Parmesan cheese

Prepare crepes according to any basic recipe.

For filling, saute onion in butter in a large skillet until soft. Stir in ham, tomato, basil, fennel and pepper. Cook and stir over low heat until liquid has almost evaporated. Remove from heat; stir in parsley.

Fill crepes, putting about 2 teaspoons filling and 1 tablespoon Swiss cheese near edge. Roll up part way, fold in sides, then roll up completely, envelope fashion. Place crepes on baking sheet (crepes can be covered and refrigerated for several hours at this point); brush tops with melted butter and sprinkle with Parmesan cheese.

Broil about 4 inches from heat for 2 minutes or until lightly browned. Cut each in half diagonally. Yields 32 appetizer crepes.

— GLACIER BAY COUNTRY INN,
GUSTAVUS

LIGHT OYSTERS ROCKEFELLER

1 lb. spinach

2 C. watercress

2 medium shallots, peeled and
  minced

1 medium clove garlic, minced

1/2 C. nonfat evaporated milk

1/2 C. fresh bread crumbs

1 T. lemon peel, grated

1/2 C. parsley, finely chopped

2 T. lemon juice

1/2 t. salt

freshly ground pepper

24 fresh oysters

1/2 C. grated low cholesterol
  Swiss cheese

2 T. safflower oil or melted
  margarine

Bring large pan of water to a boil, add spinach and watercress and blanch 3 minutes. Drain and rinse with cold water. Press out any excess liquid. Coarsely chop greens and drain again on paper towels.

In medium saucepan combine blanched greens, shallots, garlic, evaporated milk, 1 tablespoon bread crumbs and lemon peel. Bring to boil, then reduce and simmer 5 minutes.

Transfer to food processor and add parsley, lemon juice and salt and pepper to taste. Process to puree. Transfer to bowl and cool slightly. Shuck oysters, leaving meat in deeper half of shell. Place in 2 large baking pans and top each with 2 tablespoons spinach mixture. Sprinkle with cheese and remaining bread crumbs; drizzle oil or melted margarine over tops. Place oysters under hot broiler 6 inches from heat, broil 5 minutes until bubbling and brown. Serve immediately. Serves 8.

— **ARCTIC TERN B & B,**
SOLDOTNA

OYSTERS ROCKEFELLER

1/4 C. shallots, chopped

1/3 C. celery, chopped

4 sprigs fresh parsley

1/2 t. dried tarragon, crushed

1 C. fresh spinach, chopped

1/2 C. soft bread crumbs

1 C. butter, softened

1 t. anchovy paste

1 T. Worcestershire sauce

ground black pepper

salt

3 dozen fresh oysters in shell

rock salt

3/4 C. grated Gruyere cheese

In food processor fitted with steel blade, process shallots, celery, parsley, tarragon and spinach until chopped. Add bread crumbs, softened butter, anchovy paste, Worcestershire sauce and 1/2 teaspoon salt. Season to taste with pepper. Pulse until mixed. Season to taste with salt.

Shuck oysters leaving them in deeper shell. Place rock salt in bottom of 6 aluminum pie plates. Set 6 oysters on top of rock salt in each pan. Place 1 tablespoon spinach and bread crumb mixture to cover each oyster and sprinkle lightly with cheese. Bake at 425 degrees for 5 or 6 minutes, or until sauce bubbles. Then place under hot broiler 2 minutes longer to brown cheese slightly. To serve, transfer oysters with rock salt to serving plates. Serves 6.

— ARCTIC TERN B & B,
SOLDOTNA

PICKLED FISH

1/2 gal. firm, white fish

1 1/4 C. pickling salt

1 qt. cider vinegar

Lots of sliced onion rings

Syrup:

1 qt. white vinegar

2 C. sugar

1/2 box pickling spice

Cut fish in bite-sized pieces. Mix fish, pickling salt and cider vinegar and place in a 1-gallon jar. Use enough vinegar to cover fish. Soak 5 to 7 days in refrigerator, stirring daily. Drain and rinse thoroughly in cold water. Rinse out jar; add drained fish and onions. Heat vinegar, sugar, pickling spice until sugar dissolves. Pour over fish and sliced onions. Cover and let stand in refrigerator for 1 week to marinate before serving. Will keep in the refrigerator for several months.

— **W. T. FUGARWE LODGE, GUSTAVUS**

PICKLED MUSHROOMS

1 envelope Italian dressing mix

1/3 C. tarragon or rice vinegar

2 T. water

2/3 C. salad oil

1 T. sugar

4 cloves crushed garlic

6 drops Tabasco sauce

1 medium onion, thinly sliced

2 4-oz. cans button mushrooms, drained

Shake together Italian dressing mix, vinegar and water in tightly covered jar. Add oil, sugar, garlic and Tabasco sauce. Cover and shake to mix. Add mushrooms and onion rings. Cover and refrigerate at least 8 hours.

— **ARCTIC TERN B & B, SOLDOTNA**

STUFFED MUSHROOMS ILIASKA

12 to 16 fresh mushrooms

1/4 C. butter

3 T. chopped green pepper

3 T. finely chopped onion

1/2 C. fresh bread crumbs

1 C. Polish sausage, ground or
    finely chopped

dash of cayenne pepper

Clean mushrooms with a damp cloth, remove stems. Chop stems and saute in butter with green pepper and onion. Add fresh bread crumbs, sausage and cayenne; stuff mushrooms with mixture. Place in greased shallow pan. Bake at 350 degrees for about 15 minutes. Makes 6 to 8 servings.

— **ILIASKA LODGE,
ILIAMNA LAKE**

SMOKED SALMON DIP

1 lb. smoked salmon, broken
    into pieces

10 oz. cream cheese, softened

1 C. mayonnaise

a few drops liquid smoke

a few drops Tabasco sauce
    (optional)

chives, chopped (garnish)

crackers or garlic toast points

Combine smoked salmon, cream cheese, mayonnaise, liquid smoke and Tabasco (if using), mixing until smooth; sprinkle with chopped chives and serve in a bowl surrounded by crackers and/or toast points.

— **ALASKA RAINBOW LODGE,
KING SALMON**

SPICY SALMON DIP

1 C. flaked salmon

3 oz. cream cheese

1 C. mayonnaise

1 T. lemon juice

1/3 C. chili sauce

2 T. horseradish

2 T. chopped green onion

1 T. sweet pickle relish

Beat first 4 ingredients together until creamy, then add remaining ingredients and mix well.

— ARCTIC TERN B & B,
SOLDOTNA

DAFFODIL DIP

8 oz. cream cheese

2 hard boiled eggs

2 T. minced chives or red onion

1/4 to 1/2 t. garlic powder

1/3 C. mayonnaise

Mix all ingredients. Refrigerate and serve with vegetables.

— ARCTIC TERN B & B,
SOLDOTNA

BAKED BRIE AND GARLIC

4 large heads of garlic

1/3 C. olive oil

1 t. salt

4 4-oz. wheels Brie cheese

1 baguette French bread (narrow

loaf of French bread)

Remove outer skins from the garlic and break up the cloves. Arrange the cloves closely in an oven-proof dish. Drizzle the olive oil across the top.

Sprinkle with salt. Cover with foil and bake at 350 degrees for 1 to 1 1/2 hours. Preheat the broiler. Score a large X on top of each wheel of Brie. Place wheels in an oven-proof dish and broil until bubbly.

Serve the cheese and garlic immediately with baguette slices. Makes 8 servings.

— **RIVERSONG LODGE,
YENTNA RIVER**

CHEESE BALL

16 oz. cream cheese, room

temperature

8 oz. Cheddar cheese, shredded

1 T. pimento, chopped

1 T. green pepper, chopped

1 T. onion, finely chopped

2 t. Worcestershire sauce

dash cayenne pepper

dash salt

Mix cream cheese and all other ingredients together. Shape into a ball and roll in chopped nuts or chopped parsley.

— **DAYBREAK B & B
FAIRBANKS**

CHEESE NUT PATE

1 C. minced onion

1 T. butter

1 C. almonds and/or walnuts,
　ground fine

8 oz. cream cheese

16 oz. cottage cheese

1/2 t. salt

1 t. fresh ground black pepper

1/2 t. dill weed

2 t. prepared mustard

1 T. lemon juice

2 C. packed grated Cheddar
　cheese

1 C. ricotta cheese (optional)

parsley, finely minced (optional)

Grease a 9- x 4-inch loaf pan. Saute onions in butter until limp. Mix remaining ingredients (except ricotta and parsley) with onions in a food processor until well blended. Spread mixture into greased loaf pan and bake 1 hour at 325 degrees (mixture will firm as it cools). Cool and chill.

Unmold onto serving platter. If desired, spread top and sides with ricotta and sprinkle with parsley to decorate. Serve with dark rye bread, toasted French bread or crackers. Serves 12.

— **RIVERSONG LODGE,
YENTNA RIVER**

GUACAMOLE

8 avocadoes, mashed

16 oz. lite cream cheese

1 tomato, finely chopped

20 drops Tabasco

4 green onions, chopped

2 4-oz. cans green chilies

juice of one lemon

Combine all ingredients. Chill and serve with corn or tortilla chips. Recipe may be halved.

— **ALL THE COMFORTS OF
HOME, ANCHORAGE**

PINEAPPLE-CREAM CHEESE BALL

2 8-oz. pkgs. cream cheese

1 10-oz. can crushed pineapple, drained

1 large onion, chopped or grated

1 large bell pepper, chopped fine

dash of hot sauce

1 C. pecans, chopped

Mix all ingredients except pecans. Shape into ball and chill overnight. Roll in pecans before serving.

— WINDSOCK INN,
JUNEAU

SALMON SPREAD

1 1/2 lb. salmon

1 1/2 C. butter

1/2 t. Worcestershire sauce

1 1/2 T. Dijon mustard

1 t. catsup

1/4 C. lemon juice

dash Tabasco sauce

1/8 t. nutmeg

1/8 t. curry powder

1 T. onion, minced

Poach salmon; remove skin and bones. Mix salmon and butter in food processor until well blended. Add remaining ingredients and process until well mixed. Serve with crackers. Will keep for 1 week covered and refrigerated. Makes 3 cups; serves 12.

— RIVERSONG LODGE,
YENTNA RIVER

HERBED BREAD STICKS

1 small loaf white bread, sliced
    with crusts removed

1/4 t. salt

1/4 t. pepper

1 large clove garlic, chopped

1/2 C. butter, softened

1/4 C. Parmesan cheese, grated

2 T. fresh chives, chopped

1 T. fresh marjoram or other
    herbs, chopped

butter, melted

Roll each bread slice flat with a rolling pin. Set aside. Mash salt, pepper, and garlic with the back of a spoon. Stir in butter, cheese, and herbs; spread one side of each bread slice with the mixture. Roll up jelly-roll fashion and secure with a toothpick. Place, seam side down, on a baking sheet. Brush lightly with butter. Bake at 350 degrees for 12 to 15 minutes or until browned,. turning several times. Makes about 20 bread sticks. Serve with a smoked salmon dip spread on small slices of very fresh cucumber.

**—RIVERSONG LODGE,
YENTNA RIVER**

DRINKS ON THE HOUSE

RHUBARB LEMONADE

3 C. rhubarb, cut in small pieces

3 C. water

1 1/4 C. sugar

1/2 C. lemon juice

1 16-oz. bottle (2 C.) lemon-lime
   carbonated drink

lemon slices

Ice ring (optional):

lemon slices

whole strawberries

mint leaves

borage flowers

Combine rhubarb and water in saucepan; bring to boil. Cover and simmer 10 minutes. Cool; squeeze through cheesecloth to extract the juice. Add sugar, return to heat. Simmer and stir until sugar is thoroughly dissolved. Remove from heat and stir in lemon juice. Chill.

Just before serving, pour syrup over ice cubes; pour in carbonated beverage. Garnish with lemon slices or pour into punch bowl over ice ring for open house, weddings, etc.

Ice ring: Arrange lemon slices vertically in ring mold. Put strawberries between lemon slices. Arrange mint leaves and borage flowers around top. Pour rhubarb lemonade over all and freeze until firm. Place mold in pan of hot water briefly to loosen; invert mold.

—**GLACIER BAY COUNTRY INN,
GUSTAVUS**

WAKE-UP SHAKE

1 1/2 C. skim milk

1 C. flavored yogurt, chilled

2 ripe medium bananas, peeled, halved, and frozen

1/2 C. orange juice, chilled

In a blender container combine all ingredients. Cover and blend until smooth. Serve in tall glasses. Makes 2 servings.

—ANCHOR RIVER B & B, ANCHOR POINT

FROSTY ORANGE JUICE

orange juice

3 bananas, peeled and frozen

ice cubes

Fill blender three-fourths full of orange juice. Add bananas and ice cubes. When breakfast is ready, blend until frothy and serve immediately.

—BLUEBERRY LODGE B & B, JUNEAU

HOT SPICED WINE

1/2 gallon apple juice

1/2 stick cinnamon

8 whole cloves

1 T. grated orange peel

lemon juice, if desired

burgundy wine

Simmer first 5 ingredients for 20 to 30 minutes. (Can let set all night). Add burgundy to taste. Warm and serve.

This is good on cold winter days.

—FAVORITE BAY INN, ANGOON

BERRY BOUNCE

fresh berries (salmonberries,
    blueberries, raspberries, etc.)

4 C. sugar

1 fifth vodka, brandy or gin

Wash and sterilize a large 1-gallon glass jar and lid; cool jar. Fill jar about one-quarter full with fresh berries, sprinkle with 1 cup of the sugar. Keep layering berries gently with the sugar—do not press the berries down—until you reach the top and all sugar is used up.

Pour the liquor of your choice over the berries, leaving at least 1 inch of headroom at the top. Screw lid on firmly and set on counter. For the next 4 days, the jar should be picked up and bounced up and down at least twice a day. After the fifth day, place the jar on the shelf to age for at least 30 days. Strain a few times through cheesecloth and enjoy.

**—GLACIER BAY COUNTRY INN,
GUSTAVUS**

SANGRIA

1/2 C. lemon juice

1/2 C. orange juice

1/2 C. sugar

1/4 C. brandy

1 C. sliced fruit

1 4/5-qt. bottle dry red or white
    wine

1 7-oz. bottle club soda

1 tray of ice

Mix lemon juice, orange juice, sugar and brandy. Add fruit. Refrigerate for several hours. At serving time, pour fruit mixture into small punch bowl. Add wine, club soda and ice. Stir and serve. Serves 8.

**—WINDSOCK INN B & B,
DOUGLAS**

VERY BERRY BRANDY

4 C. sugar

2 C. water

3 C. fresh berries (see note)

2 C. brandy

1 t. grated orange zest

1 t. grated lemon zest

10 whole allspice

5 whole cloves

Combine sugar and water in a heavy pan. Stir to mix. Heat to boiling, reduce the heat and simmer until sugar has dissolved. Remove from heat. Cool syrup to room temperature.

Combine berries, brandy, 1/2 cup simple syrup, orange and lemon zests, allspice, and cloves in a 2-quart glass container. (**Note:** Use a single kind of berry—blueberries work well but others can be substituted. If you use blueberries, pierce them lightly with a fork.) Cover with plastic wrap and place in a cool, dark place for 2 weeks, stirring every 3 days.

Drain the berries in a sieve set over a large measuring bowl. Press against the berries with the back of a wooden spoon to get out as much juice as possible. Strain the juice through a clean sieve lined with damp cheesecloth into a clean container. The idea is to keep straining the juice to get it as clear as possible. Keep going back and forth with clean cheesecloth or try using a funnel lined with a moistened clean paper or coffee filter. When the juice looks nice and clear, test for sweetness. Add more of the syrup mixture as needed. Let the final product sit in a cool, dark place for 3 to 4 weeks, filter again into a pretty bottle and enjoy! Makes about 3 cups.

**—RIVERSONG LODGE,
YENTNA RIVER**

CHAPTER 2

Fresh from the Oven

COFFEECAKES

RASPBERRY RHUBARB COFFEECAKE

Filling:

3 C. rhubarb and raspberries

2 T. lemon juice

Cake:

3 C. flour

1 C. sugar

1 t. salt

1 t. baking powder

1 t. baking soda

1 C. butter

1 C. buttermilk

2 eggs (slightly beaten)

1 t. vanilla

Topping:

3/4 C. sugar

1/2 C. flour

1/4 C. butter

Cook filling ingredients 5 minutes; let cool.

Cake: Combine dry ingredients and cut in butter. Beat together buttermilk, eggs, and vanilla and add to dry ingredients, mixing just until moist. Spread half the batter in a greased 9- x 13-inch pan. Spread rhubarb/raspberry mixture over and spoon remaining batter on top in small mounds.

Topping: Cut butter into dry ingredients until mixture is fine crumbs. Sprinkle over batter and bake at 350 degrees for 40 to 45 minutes.

—McCARTHY WILDERNESS
B & B, McCARTHY

OVERNIGHT COFFEECAKE

3/4 C. shortening

1 C. sugar

2 eggs

6 oz. sour cream

2 C. flour

1 t. baking powder

1 t. baking soda

1 t. nutmeg

1/2 t. salt

3/4 C. brown sugar

1/2 C. walnuts

1 t. cinnamon

Cream shortening and sugar until light and fluffy. Add eggs and sour cream and mix well. Sift together flour, baking powder, baking soda, nutmeg and salt. Add to batter and mix well. Pour batter into greased 9- x 13-inch pan. Mix brown sugar, walnuts and cinnamon. Sprinkle over the batter. Cover and chill overnight. In the morning uncover and bake at 350 degrees 35 to 40 minutes or until cake tests done.

—THE SUMMER INN B & B, HAINES

PECAN COFFEECAKE

3/4 C. pecans, finely chopped

1/4 C. brown sugar

3 C. Bisquick baking mix

1 C. sugar

1 1/2 C. plain yogurt

1/4 C. margarine, softened

1 1/2 t. vanilla

3 egg whites

Grease and flour 12-cup bundt cake pan. Mix pecans and brown sugar; set aside. Mix remaining ingredients and spread half in pan; sprinkle pecan mixture on top. Spread remaining batter over filling. Bake at 350 degrees until wooden toothpick inserted in the center comes out clean, 45 to 50 minutes.

—CAMAI B & B, ANCHORAGE

LINGONBERRY (LOWBUSH CRANBERRY) COFFEECAKE

2 C. flour

3/4 t. salt

1/2 C. butter

1/2 C. milk

3 t. baking powder

1/2 C. sugar

1 egg

2 C. lingonberries (see note)

1/2 C. butter

1/2 C. flour

1 C. sugar

Mix first 7 ingredients; fold in berries. Spread in greased 9- x 12-inch pan. Make topping by cutting butter into flour and sugar. Sprinkle topping over cake batter.

Bake at 375 degrees for 30 to 35 minutes.

Note: Frozen cranberries may be substituted for lingonberries.

**—DAYBREAK B & B,
FAIRBANKS**

BLUEBERRY BREAKFAST CAKE

2 C. biscuit mix

1/4 C. sugar

1 egg

1 C. sour cream

1 C. blueberries

1/4 C. sugar

1/2 t. cinnamon

1 T. butter

Combine biscuit mix, sugar, egg and sour cream. Beat by hand for one minute. Fold in blueberries. Spread in well buttered, 8- x 8- x 2-inch pan. With pastry blender, mix sugar, cinnamon and butter. Sprinkle on cake. Bake at 400 degrees for 30 minutes; serve warm.

**—WALLIN'S HILLTOP B & B,
ANCHOR POINT**

STREUSEL-FILLED COFFEECAKE

3/4 C. sugar

1/4 C. soft shortening

1 egg

1 1/2 C. flour

2 t. baking powder

1/2 t. salt

1/2 C. milk

1 t. vanilla

Streusel topping:

1/2 C. brown sugar

2 T. flour

2 t. cinnamon

2 T. butter

1/2 C. nuts

Cream sugar and shortening; add egg and mix well. Sift flour, baking powder and salt and add alternately with milk to creamed mixture. Add vanilla. Spread half of batter in 9- x 9- x 1 3/4-inch greased and floured pan. Mix topping ingredients. Sprinkle over batter in pan then spread the remaining batter on top. Bake at 350 degrees for 25 minutes.

—GREAT ALASKA CEDAR WORKS B & B, KETCHIKAN

M U F F I N S

APPLE, CINNAMON AND RAISIN MUFFINS

2 C. flour

2/3 C. dark brown sugar, packed

1 T. baking powder

1/2 t. freshly grated nutmeg

1 egg

1/3 C. safflower oil

2/3 C. unsweetened apple juice

1 tart cooking apple, shredded

1 t. cinnamon

1/2 C. raisins

1/2 C. pecans or walnuts,
    chopped

Generously butter 12 muffin cups, each 2 1/2 inches in diameter. In large bowl, sift together flour, brown sugar, baking powder, and nutmeg. In another medium bowl, combine egg, oil, and apple juice. Whisk until blended. In medium bowl, toss together apple and cinnamon until evenly coated. Stir in raisins and nuts.

Pour egg mixture over sifted dry ingredients and fold lightly 3 or 4 times with a rubber spatula to partially combine. Add apple mixture and distribute evenly, using as few strokes as possible (batter should not be perfectly smooth).

Quickly divide batter among prepared muffin cups. Bake in middle of a 400-degree oven for about 25 minutes, or until tops of muffins are golden and spring back when lightly pressed. Let muffins cool in pan for about 2 minutes. Using a blunt knife, ease muffins onto a wire rack and let cool for 15 to 20 minutes. Makes 12 muffins.

**—WASILLA LAKE B & B,
WASILLA**

APPLESAUCE BRAN MUFFINS

4 eggs

1 1/2 C. oil

1 1/4 C. brown sugar

1/4 C. molasses

1 C. raisins

2 C. applesauce

3 C. flour

1 t. soda

1 1/2 T. baking powder

1/2 t. salt

1 T. cinnamon

2 C. natural wheat bran

Grease 24 muffin tins. Mix liquid ingredients in large bowl. Add dry ingredients and stir. Bake at 350 degrees for 20 to 25 minutes. Makes 2 dozen hearty and delicious muffins. You may substitute oats for some of the bran.

—CLAY'S QUALITY B & B,
HOMER

APPLESAUCE RAISIN MUFFINS

1 large egg

2 T. vegetable oil

1 1/2 C. unsweetened applesauce

2 C. flour

2 T. sugar

1/2 t. cinnamon

3/4 t. baking soda

2 t. baking powder

1/2 t. nutmeg

3/4 C. raisins

Beat together egg, oil and applesauce. Add flour, sugar, baking soda, baking powder and spices. Beat well. Stir in raisins. Spoon batter onto floured and oiled muffin tins. Bake at 375 degrees for 20 to 25 minutes or until firm to touch and browned. Cool on wire rack. Delicious topped with cream cheese. Makes 12.

—ARCTIC TERN B & B,
SOLDOTNA

BANANA BRAN MUFFINS

1 C. mashed ripe bananas
  (2 medium bananas)

1 egg or egg substitute

1/4 C. molasses

2 T. oil

2/3 C. skim milk

1/2 C. oat bran

1/4 C. wheat germ

1 C. whole wheat flour

1 t. baking soda

1/4 t. cinnamon

Combine banana and liquids in large bowl. Stir together dry ingredients, breaking up any lumps. Stir dry ingredients into banana mixture. Mix just until dry ingredients are moistened. Spoon into greased muffin tins, filling 3/4 full. Bake 15 to 18 minutes at 375 degrees. Makes 12 large or 15 medium muffins, heavy and moist. Nuts and raisins can be added.

**—ARCTIC TERN B & B,
SOLDOTNA**

BANANA MUFFINS

3 ripe bananas, mashed

2 t. baking soda

1 C. mayonnaise

1 C. sugar

2 C. flour

2 t. cinnamon

1/2 C. walnuts or 2 t. poppy or
  sunflower seeds (optional)

Sprinkle baking soda over ripe bananas and let rest at least 10 minutes. Add mayonnaise, sugar, flour, cinnamon, and optional seeds or nuts. Use paper inserts in muffin tins and fill 3/4 full. Bake 25 minutes at 375 degrees. Makes 24.

**—BENTLEY'S PORTER
HOUSE B & B, BETHEL**

BARANOF POPPY SEED MUFFINS

3 C. flour

2 1/4 C. sugar

1 1/2 t. baking powder

1 1/2 t. salt

1 1/2 T. poppy seeds

1 1/2 C. peanut oil

1 1/2 C. buttermilk

3 eggs

1/2 t. almond extract

Preheat oven to 350 degrees. Grease 2 12-cup muffin tins. Combine dry ingredients in large bowl. Combine wet ingredients and add to dry ingredients until just moistened. Bake 30 minutes. Makes 24.

—BARANOF WILDERNESS LODGE, AUKE BAY

BRAN MUFFINS

3 C. bran

1 C. boiling water

2 eggs

1 C. honey

1/2 C. oil

2 C. buttermilk or 3 C. yogurt

2 C. whole wheat flour

2 1/2 t. soda

1/2 C. white flour

1/2 t. salt

Mix bran and water in a large bowl and let stand. Beat the eggs, honey, oil and buttermilk or yogurt together and add to the bran. Sift dry ingredients and add to the bran mixture.

Spoon batter into greased muffin tins. Bake at 375 degrees for 18 minutes. Makes 24.

Variation: Raisins or nuts may be added.

—THE CHALET B & B, KENAI

CRANBERRY STREUSEL MUFFINS

1 C. flour

1/2 C. whole wheat flour

2 t. baking powder

1/2 t. baking soda

1/4 t. salt

3/4 C. sugar

2/3 C. buttermilk

1 stick unsalted butter

2 large eggs

1 1/2 C. frozen cranberries

Streusel topping:

1/4 C. sugar

3 T. flour

1 T. unsalted butter, chilled

1/2 t. cinnamon

pinch of salt

Topping: My favorite way to make streusel is to use a food processor to mix all the ingredients quickly. The butter should be cold so the topping is crumbly. Place all the ingredients into the processor bowl and pulse for 10 to 15 seconds. If you don't have a food processor, use a pastry blender or two knives. Set the topping aside.

Muffins: Coarsely chop the cranberries. Butter 12 1/2-cup muffin cups. Set aside. Mix well all of the other ingredients except for the berries. Gently stir the berries into the batter. Fill each muffin cup 2/3 full. Sprinkle the tops generously with the streusel topping.

Bake in the center of the oven at 375 degrees for 25 minutes or until the muffins are firm to touch and the tops are golden brown. Cool in pans 5 minutes, then remove to a wire rack. Serve warm. Makes 12.

—RIVERSONG LODGE,
YENTNA RIVER

LINGONBERRY (LOWBUSH CRANBERRY) MUFFINS

3/4 C. lingonberries

3/4 C. powdered sugar

2 C. flour

3 t. baking powder

1 t. salt

1/4 C. sugar

1 egg

1 C. milk

4 T. shortening, melted

Mix berries with powdered sugar and set aside. Sift dry ingredients and add egg, milk and shortening all at once. Mix only until dry ingredients are moist. Fold in berries. Fill muffin tins 2/3 full. Bake at 350 degrees for 20 minutes. Makes 12.

I like to serve these warm for breakfast. I pick the wild berries in the fall just after the first frost and freeze a supply for making these delicious muffins year round.

—MARLOW'S KENAI RIVER B & B, SOLDOTNA

MANDARIN MUFFINS

1 11-oz. can mandarin orange
  segments

1 T. orange extract

2 t. baking soda

1/2 t. salt

1/4 C. sugar

2 C. flour

2 t. baking powder

1/2 C. brown sugar

1 egg

1 8-oz. carton sour cream

1/3 C. shortening, melted

Drain oranges, reserving liquid. Cut segments into halves. Add orange extract to reserved liquid and add to oranges.

Combine dry ingredients in a large bowl. In a separate bowl, mix egg, sour cream and shortening; add to dry ingredients. Add oranges and juice and mix just until moistened. Spoon into greased or paper-lined muffin tins, filling 2/3 full. Bake at 400 degrees for 20 to 25 minutes.

**—FAIRBANKS DOWNTOWN
B & B, FAIRBANKS**

MY FAVORITE MUFFINS

1 15-oz. box raisin bran

5 C. flour

6 t. baking soda

2 t. salt

3 C. sugar

1 qt. buttermilk

1 C. oil

4 eggs, beaten

Mix all dry ingredients. Add buttermilk, oil and eggs. Mix well. Fill greased muffin tins 3/4 full. Bake at 400 degrees for 15 to 20 minutes. These muffins stay moist for several days, and the batter will keep in the refrigerator for up to 6 weeks in a covered jar.

**—ANCHOR RIVER B & B,
ANCHOR POINT**

OAT BRAN MUFFINS

2 C. oat bran

2 t. baking powder

1 C. nonfat milk

2 egg whites

1/3 C. molasses

2 T. vegetable oil

3/4 C. raisins

Line 10 medium muffin cups with paper liners. Stir together oat bran and baking powder. Add milk, egg whites, molasses and oil. Mix until dry ingredients are moist. Stir in raisins. Fill muffin cups 7/8 full. Bake at 425 degrees for 15 minutes or until golden brown. Serve with honey.

—CAMAI B & B,
ANCHORAGE

PECAN ORANGE MUFFINS

peel from 1 medium orange

1/2 C. butter

1 C. sugar

2 eggs

1 t. baking soda

2 C. flour

1 C. plain yogurt

3/4 C. pecans, finely chopped

1/3 C. fresh squeezed orange
    juice

1 T. sugar

Grease muffin tins. Finely grate orange peel. Beat butter and sugar with electric mixer until creamy. Beat in eggs; stir in baking soda and grated peel. Fold in half of the flour, then half of the yogurt. Repeat, then fold in pecans. Spoon batter into cups. Bake at 375 degrees 20 to 25 minutes. Remove from oven. Brush or spoon orange juice over hot muffins and sprinkle with 1 tablespoon sugar. Makes 12.

—ALASKA'S 7 GABLES B & B,
FAIRBANKS

POPPY SEED MUFFINS

2 C. flour

2 1/2 t. baking powder

2 T. sugar

3/4 t. salt

1/2 C. oil

1 egg beaten

3/4 C. milk

1/2 t. vanilla

3 t. poppy seeds

Mix all ingredients and pour into individual muffin tins, greased and floured, or lined with papers. Bake at 400 degrees for 20 to 25 minutes.

—TALBOTT'S B & B,
DELTA JUNCTION

POPPY SEED POUNDCAKE MUFFINS

2 C. flour

3 t. poppy seeds

1/2 t. salt

1/4 t. baking soda

1 C. sugar

1/2 C. butter

2 eggs

1 C. plain yogurt

1 t. vanilla

Mix flour, poppy seeds, salt and soda. Cream sugar and butter until fluffy. Add eggs, yogurt and vanilla. Stir in flour mixture. Moisten thoroughly— don't overmix.

Bake at 400 degrees for 15 to 20 minutes.

—BLUEBERRY LODGE B & B
DOUGLAS

QUIET PLACE BLUEBERRY MUFFINS

2 C. flour

4 t. baking powder

1/2 t. salt

1/2 C. sugar

1 C. fresh or frozen blueberries

1 egg, beaten

1/4 C. melted shortening

1 C. milk

Sift dry ingredients together and stir in berries. Mix egg, shortening and milk; add to dry ingredients and stir just until mixed. Fill greased muffin tins 2/3 full. Bake at 400 degrees for 20 to 25 minutes. Makes 18.

—QUIET PLACE LODGE, HALIBUT COVE

RICH LEMON MUFFINS

2 C. all-purpose flour

1/2 C. sugar

1 T. baking powder

1 t. salt

1 stick butter

1/2 C. fresh lemon juice

2 eggs

finely grated rind of 1 lemon

Blend first 4 ingredients well. Melt butter, remove from heat and stir in lemon juice, eggs and lemon rind. Stir liquid mixture into dry ingredients and mix until well moistened. Spoon batter into buttered muffins cups and sprinkle with sugar. Bake at 400 degrees for 15 to 20 minutes until lightly browned. Serve with fruit platter.

—FRANCINE'S B & B, HOMER

Six-Week Muffins

1 C. boiling water

1 C. raisins

2 1/2 t. baking soda

1/2 C. shortening

1 C. sugar

2 eggs, beaten until thick

2 C. All Bran

1 C. Bran Flakes

2 1/2 C. flour

1/2 t. salt

2 C. buttermilk

Combine water, raisins and baking soda; let cool. Cream shortening and sugar, then stir in eggs. Add remaining ingredients and mix well. Stir in water and raisin mixture.

Store covered in refrigerator. Use as needed. Bake 20 minutes at 350 degrees. This will keep 6 weeks. Never re-mix the batter—just spoon out the amount needed from the top.

—LISIANSKI LODGE, PELICAN

Sour Cream Poppy Seed Muffins

2 C. flour

1/4 C. poppy seeds

1/2 t. salt

1/2 C. softened butter

3/4 C. sugar

2 eggs

1/4 t. baking soda

1 t. vanilla

3/4 C. sour cream

Generously grease 12 muffin cups. Mix flour, poppy seeds, salt and baking soda in a medium bowl. Cream butter and sugar until light and fluffy. Add eggs and beat well. Fold in sour cream and vanilla. Add to dry ingredients and mix just until combined. Spoon into muffin cups and bake at 400 degrees 15 to 20 minutes.

—SPRUCE ACRES B & B CABINS, HOMER

FRENCH BREAKFAST PUFFS

1/3 C. shortening

1/2 C. sugar

1 egg

1 1/2 C. flour

1 1/2 t. baking powder

1/2 t. salt

1/4 t. nutmeg

1/2 C. milk

1/2 C. sugar

1 t. cinnamon

1/2 C. butter, melted

Grease 15 medium muffin cups or 12 large muffin cups. Mix thoroughly shortening, sugar, and egg. Combine flour, baking powder, salt and nutmeg; add to egg mixture, alternating with the milk. Fill muffin cups 2/3 full. Bake at 350 degrees 20 to 25 minutes until golden brown. Mix 1/2 cup sugar and the cinnamon. Immediately after baking, roll hot muffins in melted butter and then in the cinnamon-sugar mixture. Serve warm.

**—BOWEY'S B & B,
KETCHIKAN**

B R E A D S

GIANT STRAWBERRY SCONE

3 C. flour

2 t. lemon peel, grated

3/4 C. sugar

1/2 t. baking powder

1 t. baking soda

1/2 C. butter

1 C. buttermilk

6 C. strawberries, washed and
   drained

steamed milk or whipped cream

Cut butter into dry ingredients (including lemon peel) until crumbly. Add buttermilk and stir just until moistened. Scrape dough onto floured board and knead 10 times. Pat into a round and place in a greased 9-inch cake pan. Sprinkle with sugar. Bake at 400 degrees for 35 minutes.

Slice strawberries and stir in 1 tablespoon sugar. When scone has cooled, slice horizontally, and carefully lift off top. Fill the scone with strawberries, replace top and serve in wedges. Pass steamed milk or whipped cream.

—BLUEBERRY LODGE B & B,
DOUGLAS

CARDAMOM-PRUNE DROP SCONES

2 C. flour

2 t. baking powder

1/2 t. baking soda

1/4 t. salt

3/4 t. ground cardamom seeds

8 T. unsalted butter

3/4 C. finely cut, moist prunes

3/4 C. sour cream

1 large egg

1/4 C. granulated sugar

1 t. freshly grated lemon peel

Mix flour, baking powder, baking soda, salt and cardamom seeds in large bowl. Add butter to the flour mixture and cut in. Add prunes and toss to distribute evenly. In another bowl, beat sour cream, egg, sugar and lemon peel until well blended. Add to flour mixture and stir with a spoon until a sticky dough forms. Drop 1/3 cupfuls of dough 2 inches apart on an ungreased cookie sheet. Bake at 375 degrees 20 to 25 minutes, until golden brown.

**—BEACH HOUSE B & B,
HOMER**

SCALLION BISCUITS

2 C. flour

5 t. baking powder

2 T. butter

1 C. milk (scant)

1/2 t. salt

1/3 C. chopped scallions

Mix dry ingredients and work in butter with pastry cutter until well incorporated, add only enough milk to make a soft and supple dough. Mix in the scallions and roll out 1/2-inch thick on floured surface. Cut out with biscuit cutter, put on a greased cookie sheet and bake 12 to 15 minutes at 425 degrees until golden brown.

—RIVERSONG LODGE, YENTNA RIVER

MILE-HIGH BISCUITS

2 C. flour

1 C. whole wheat flour

4 1/2 t. baking powder

2 T. sugar

1/2 t. salt

3/4 t. cream of tartar

3/4 C. butter

1 egg, beaten

1 C. milk

Mix all ingredients until smooth. Roll onto floured surface and cut into circles. Bake at 450 degrees for 12 to 15 minutes until golden.

—BOWEY'S B & B, KETCHIKAN

KATHIE'S BAGELS

2 T. yeast

1 1/2 C. warm water

3 T. sugar

1 T. salt

4 1/2 C. flour (approximate)

Dissolve yeast in the warm water. In a large bowl combine yeast mixture, sugar, salt and 1 1/2 cups of the flour. Beat at low speed in mixer for half a minute. Beat at high speed for 3 minutes. Stir in 2 3/4 to 3 cups flour by hand to make a stiff dough. Knead 8 to 10 minutes, cover and let rest 15 minutes. Cut into 12 portions and shape into balls. Punch hole in center and pull to enlarge circle. Cover and let rise 20 minutes.

In a large kettle, bring 1 gallon water and 1 tablespoon sugar to a boil. Simmer 4 bagels at a time for 7 minutes, turning once. Drain and place on a greased cookie sheet. Bake at 350 degrees for 30 minutes.

**—REDOUBT VIEW B & B,
SOLDOTNA**

ALMOND SWEDISH RUSKS

3 C. flour (more if sticky)

1 t. baking soda

1/2 C. butter or margarine

1 C. sugar

2 eggs

1/2 C. sour cream or buttermilk

1 C. chopped almonds (optional)

Combine flour and baking soda and set aside. Melt butter and let cool. Add sugar. Beat in eggs. Stir in buttermilk or sour cream and then almonds. Stir in flour mixture. Pat into loaf shape. Bake on cookie sheet at 300 degrees for 45 minutes.

**—THE SUMMER INN B & B,
HAINES**

PULL APARTS

3 pkgs. buttermilk refrigerator
   biscuits (36 biscuits total)

1 1/2 C. brown sugar

1/4 C. water

1 1/2 cubes margarine

1 1/2 t. cinnamon

1/2 C. chopped nuts

Cut biscuits into quarters and set aside. Combine the brown sugar, water and margarine in a large skillet and bring to a full boil. Add cinnamon and nuts. Remove from heat. Fold in biscuits and stir until completely covered. Pour into large bundt pan. Bake at 375 degrees for 20 minutes. Turn onto plate and serve hot.

**—ARCTIC TERN B & B,
SOLDOTNA**

LEFSE

4 C. sour milk

1 C. sugar

1 C. Karo syrup

2 t. baking soda

1 T. melted butter

1 pinch salt

enough flour to roll out

Combine all ingredients to make a soft dough and pinch off small balls. Roll to thin sheets and bake flat in oven at 350 degrees for 1 minute. Do not brown. Stack flat and when cool store in refrigerator. When ready to serve, dip in warm water and quickly place between cloths until evenly moist. Spread with butter, sugar and cinnamon.

**—JEWELL'S BY THE SEA,
PETERSBURG**

NORWEGIAN PASTRY (KRINGLER)

Base:

1 C. flour

1 T. sugar

1/2 C. margarine or butter

1 T. water

Topping:

1 C. water

1/2 C. margarine or butter

1 C. flour

1 T. sugar

1/2 t. almond extract

3 eggs

Glaze:

1 C. powdered sugar

1 T. margarine or butter

1 T. half and half

2 t. almond extract cream

Base: In a medium bowl, combine 1 cup flour and 1 tablespoon sugar. Using pastry blender or fork, cut in 1/2 cup margarine or butter until particles are the size of small peas. Sprinkle flour mixture with 1 tablespoon water while tossing and mixing lightly with fork. Form dough into ball and divide in half. Roll or press dough into 2 14- x 3-inch rectangles on an ungreased cookie sheet.

Topping: In a medium saucepan, heat 1 cup water and 1/2 cup margarine or butter to boiling. Remove from heat. Add 1 cup flour and stir until smooth. Beat in 1 tablespoon sugar and 1/2 teaspoon almond extract. Add eggs one at a time, beating well after each addition. Spread topping mixture over base. Bake at 375 degrees for 30 to 35 minutes or until lightly browned.

Glaze: Combine glaze ingredients in a small bowl, beating until smooth. Drizzle glaze over cooked Kringler. Makes 20 servings.

—BIG EDDY B & B,
SOLDOTNA

WHIPPED STRAWBERRY POPOVERS

1 1/4 C. milk

1 1/4 C. flour

1/2 t. salt

3 jumbo eggs

strawberries

8 oz. Cool Whip

With egg beater or wire whisk, beat milk, flour and salt until well blended. Do not overbeat. Add the eggs one at a time, mixing each until completely blended. Fill popover cups 3/4 full. Do not scrape bowl. Bake at 425 degrees for 20 minutes.

Mix Cool Whip with 1/2 pint fresh strawberries or 1 package frozen strawberries, thawed and drained. Fill popovers with mixture and serve warm. (**Note:** 2 parts butter whipped with 1 part honey makes a delicious spread for popovers.)

—BRASS RING B & B,
HOMER

BANANA NUT BREAD

1/2 C. oil

1 C. sugar

2 beaten eggs

3 bananas, mashed

3 T. milk

1/2 t. vanilla

2 C. flour

1 t. baking soda

1/2 t. baking powder

1/2 t. salt

1/2 C. chopped nuts

Mix all ingredients. Pour into greased loaf pan and bake at 350 degrees for 1 hour. Remove from pan, cool and store overnight. Makes 1 loaf.

—CLAY'S QUALITY B & B,
HOMER

BLUEBERRY BREAD

2 eggs

1 C. sugar

1 C. milk

3 T. oil or melted shortening

3 C. flour

1 t. salt

4 t. baking powder

1 C. blueberries

1/2 C. nuts, chopped (optional)

Beat together eggs and sugar. Add milk and melted shortening or oil and mix well. Add flour, salt, baking powder, blueberries and nuts (if using) and stir until well blended. Pour batter into loaf pan and bake at 350 degrees for 60 minutes.

—DAYBREAK B & B, FAIRBANKS

CHOCOLATE BANANA NUT BREAD

1 1/2 C. flour

1 1/2 T. baking powder

1/4 C. unsweetened cocoa

1/2 C. butter or margarine

1 C. sugar

1 t. vanilla

2 eggs

2 ripe bananas, mashed

1/4 C. milk

1/2 C. pecans, chopped

Sift together flour, baking powder and cocoa; set aside. In mixing bowl, beat butter, sugar, and vanilla. Beat in eggs. Combine mashed bananas and milk; add the flour mixture and blend. Fold in nuts. Pour in lightly greased and floured 9- x 5- x 3-inch loaf pan. Bake at 350 degrees for 1 hour. Let cool. Dust with powdered sugar.

—ALASKA'S 7 GABLES B & B, FAIRBANKS

CHOCOLATE CHIP BANANA BREAD

2 1/2 C. flour

1/2 C. sugar

1 t. salt

1/3 C. milk

1/2 C. nuts, chopped

2/3 C. semisweet chocolate chips

1/2 C. brown sugar, packed

3 1/2 t. baking powder

3 T. vegetable oil

1 egg

1 1/4 C. bananas, mashed

Grease bottom of 9- x 5- x 3-inch loaf pan. Combine all ingredients and beat for 30 seconds. Pour into pan.

Bake at 350 degrees until wooden pick inserted in center comes out clean, 60 to 70 minutes. Cool slightly and loosen sides of loaf from pan. Remove. Cool completely before serving.

—KROTO KREEK LODGE, BIG LAKE

GOOSEBERRY NUT BREAD

1/4 C. butter or margarine

1 C. sugar

1 C. flour

1 C. whole wheat flour

1 1/2 t. baking powder

1/2 t. soda

1 T. grated orange rind

3/4 C. rhubarb juice

2 eggs

1 1/2 C. gooseberries

1/2 C. ground filberts

Cut butter or margarine into sugar. Add sifted flours, baking powder and soda. In separate bowl, combine orange rind, juice and eggs. Add to dry ingredients all at once and mix just enough to dampen. Fold in gooseberries and filberts. Pour into loaf pan and bake at 350 degrees for 1 hour.

—GOOD RIVERBED AND BREAKFAST, GUSTAVUS

GREEN CHILI CORN BREAD

1 C. cornmeal

1/2 t. salt

1/2 t. baking soda

3/4 C. milk

1/3 C. vegetable oil

2 eggs, beaten

16 oz. cream-style corn

4 oz. chopped green chilies

1 1/2 C. cheese, shredded (use Cheddar, jack or combination)

Combine cornmeal, salt and baking powder; mix well. Stir in milk and oil. Add beaten eggs and corn. Spoon half of mixture into a buttered 1 1/2-quart casserole. Sprinkle chilies and cheese on top; spoon on rest of batter. Bake at 350 degrees for 45 minutes or until toothpick inserted in center comes out clean. Serve warm.

—KACHEMAK BAY WILDERNESS LODGE, CHINA POOT BAY

JOAN'S PUMPKIN BREAD

1/2 C. oil

1 1/2 C. sugar

2 eggs

1 C. canned pumpkin

1 t. baking soda

3/4 t. cinnamon

1/2 t. cloves

1/2 C. nuts

1/3 C. water

1 3/4 C. flour

1/2 t. nutmeg

1/2 C. raisins

Combine all ingredients and mix thoroughly. Pour batter into 2 greased loaf pans and bake at 350 degrees for 1 hour.

—ALL THE COMFORTS OF HOME, ANCHORAGE

NELLIE O'LEARY'S IRISH SODA BREAD

4 C. flour

1/2 t. salt

4 t. baking powder

1 C. sugar

2 T. melted butter

1 1/2 C. raisins

2 T. caraway seeds

1/2 t. baking soda

1 1/2 C. buttermilk

1 egg, beaten

Sift together flour, salt, baking powder and sugar. Add melted butter. Stir in raisins and caraway seeds. Combine baking soda, buttermilk and beaten egg. Make a well in the center of the batter. Pour in liquid ingredients and stir into flour mixture.

Pour batter into a greased, 9-inch, cast iron frying pan. Brush lightly with milk or melted butter. Cover with aluminum foil for the first 40 minutes. Bake at 375 degrees until bread is golden brown and shrinks from the side of the pan. Test with toothpick for doneness.

My grandmother brought this recipe over from Ireland when she arrived in the United States in the early 1920's.

**—THE SUMMER INN B & B,
HAINES**

PUMPKIN BREAD

2 C. sugar

1/2 C. oil

1 egg

1 1/2 C. canned pumpkin

2 1/2 C. flour

2 t. baking soda

1/2 t. salt

1/2 t. each cinnamon, cloves
   and allspice

1/2 C. walnuts

1/2 C. dates or raisins, chopped

Blend all ingredients and mix well in large bowl.

Pour into 2 well-greased bread tins. Bake at 350 degrees for 70 minutes. Top will crack when done. Makes 2 loaves.

**—BOWEY'S B & B,
KETCHIKAN**

ZUCCHINI BREAD

2 C. sugar

3 C. flour

1 t. salt

1 t. baking soda

1/2 t. baking powder

1/4 t. allspice

1 T. cinnamon

3 eggs

1 C. oil

3 t. vanilla

2 C. grated zucchini

Mix dry ingredients; add eggs, oil and vanilla. Stir in zucchini and 1/2 cup chopped nuts, if desired. Bake in two loaf pans at 300 degrees for 1 1/2 hours. Cool pans 15 minutes before turning out.

**—ALASKA'S 7 GABLES B & B,
FAIRBANKS**

FEATHER BED ROLLS

1/2 C. shortening

4 T. sugar

1 1/2 t. salt

2 C. scalded milk

1 T. yeast

2 eggs well-beaten

4 C. flour

Place shortening, sugar and salt in bowl. Pour on scalded milk. Dissolve yeast in 1/4 cup lukewarm water. When milk mixture is lukewarm, add eggs, yeast and flour. Beat well, cover and let rise until light. Beat batter and pour into greased muffin pans. When again light, bake 10 minutes at 425 degrees. You may use half the batter and put the rest in the refrigerator, covered. When ready to use, spoon into muffin pans. Let rise until light before baking. Makes 3 dozen.

—**TUTKA BAY LODGE,**
HOMER

MELINDA'S BUTTERMILK ROLLS

2 T. dry yeast

1/4 C. honey

1 1/2 C. buttermilk (lukewarm)

1/2 C. melted butter

5 C. (about) white flour

1 t. baking soda

1 t. salt

Stir the yeast into the honey and add buttermilk, mixing until yeast is dissolved. Add the melted butter and 2 cups of the flour, the soda and the salt. Beat well and cover for 30 minutes. Stir down and add enough remaining flour to make a soft dough. Mix well, cover and let double in bulk. Punch down. Divide into small balls and place 1 inch apart on an oiled sheet. Let rise until doubled. Bake in 400-degree oven for approximately 20 minutes. Makes 24.

—**BARANOF WILDERNESS**
LODGE, AUKE BAY

OVERNIGHT CARAMEL PECAN CINNAMON ROLLS

2 pkgs. dry yeast

1/2 C. warm water (105 to 115 degrees)

2 C. lukewarm milk

1/3 C. sugar

1/3 C. oil

1 T. baking powder

2 t. salt

1 egg

6 to 8 C. flour

1/4 C. butter, softened

1/2 C. sugar

1 T. plus 1 t. cinnamon

Caramel Pecan:

1/4 C. butter, softened

1/2 C. brown sugar, packed

2 T. light corn syrup

1/2 C. pecan halves

Dissolve yeast in warm water. Stir in milk, sugar, oil, baking powder, salt, egg and 3 cups of flour. Beat until smooth. Mix in enough remaining flour to make dough easy to handle. Knead dough until smooth and elastic, 8 to 10 minutes. Place in greased bowl, turn greased side up. Cover; let rise in warm place until double, about 1 1/2 hours.

Make caramel pecan: melt butter in a 9- x 13-inch pan; stir in remaining caramel ingredients.

Punch down dough and cut in half. Roll each half into a 10- x 12-inch rectangle. Spread with 2 tablespoons of butter. Mix 1/2 cup sugar and the cinnamon; sprinkle 1/2 of the sugar mixture over dough. Roll up, beginning at 12-inch side. Pinch edge firmly to seal. Cut each roll into 12 slices. Place slightly apart in pan on top of caramel-pecan mixture. Cover and refrigerate 12 to 48 hours. Uncover and bake at 350 degrees until golden, 30 to 35 minutes. Immediately invert pan on heatproof plate and let caramel drizzle over rolls.

If desired, mix 1 C. powdered sugar, 1/2 t. vanilla and 1 T. milk until smooth. Spread over baked, warm cinnamon rolls.

—DENALI WEST LODGE,
LAKE MINCHUMINA

COCONUT BUTTER CRESCENTS

1 pkg. dry yeast

1/2 C. warm water

1/4 C. butter, softened

1/3 C. sugar

1 1/2 t. salt

1/4 t. nutmeg

1 t. grated orange peel

1/2 C. instant milk powder

3/4 C. hot water

2 C. flour

2 eggs (reserve 1 yolk)

1/2 t. vanilla

2 1/2 to 3 C. flour

1/4 C. soft butter

Filling:

1/2 C. sugar

3 T. butter

1 C. coconut

reserved egg yolk

Glaze:

1 C. powdered sugar

1/2 t. vanilla

2 to 3 T. milk

Dissolve yeast in warm water (105 to 110 degrees); set aside. Combine half the butter with the sugar, salt, nutmeg, orange peel, instant milk powder, hot water and 2 cups flour in large mixing bowl; beat until blended. Add the eggs, vanilla and dissolved yeast. Mix on low speed until blended, then beat 3 minutes on medium speed. Stir in enough of the remaining flour to make a soft dough; knead until smooth and elastic, about 10 minutes. Let rise in warm place until double, about 1 1/2 hours.

Filling: Prepare filling by beating the sugar, butter, coconut and reserved egg yolk in a small bowl. Refrigerate.

When the dough has risen, punch it down and let it rest about 10 minutes. Then roll the dough to a 14-inch square. Spread half of the dough with half of the remaining softened butter to within 2 inches of the edge. Fold in half, then in half again; seal the edges.

Again roll the dough to a 14-inch square, spread with the last of the butter, fold in half and quarters and seal. Cover and let the dough rise about 15 minutes.

Divide dough into 3 equal parts; roll each into a 9-inch circle and cut (a pizza cutter works great!) into 8 wedges. Put a teaspoon of filling in the middle of each wedge; roll up starting at the wide end. Place point side down on an ungreased baking sheet. Let rise until double, 30 to 45 minutes.

Preheat oven to 400 degrees. Bake the rolls for 10 to 12 minutes or until golden brown. Cool on rack.

Glaze: Mix powdered sugar, vanilla and milk to a spreading consistency; drizzle over rolls.

—GLACIER BAY COUNTRY INN B & B, GUSTAVUS

COUNTRY INN BRAIDED BREAD

5 to 5 1/2 C. flour

1/4 C. sugar

2 t. salt

1 pkg. dry yeast

1 1/2 C. milk

1/4 C. butter, cut in small pieces

2 eggs

1 egg white, lightly beaten with

*   1 T. water*

sesame seeds

In a large mixing bowl combine 1 cup of flour, the sugar, salt and dry yeast. Heat the milk and butter in a saucepan (or microwave) just until the milk is warm; the butter does not need to melt. Add the eggs and the warm milk mixture to the flour mixture. Mix very well until thoroughly moistened; beat on medium speed of mixer for about 3 minutes. Stir in enough of the remaining flour to make a stiff dough. Turn out onto floured board; knead the dough until it is smooth and elastic (about 5 minutes). Work into a ball; place in a greased bowl, turning to coat all sides. Cover and let rise in a warm, draft-free place until light and doubled in bulk, about 1 to 1-1/2 hours.

Punch the dough down and let rest for about 10 minutes. Divide dough into 6 equal portions. Roll each into a thin cylinder about 8 to 10 inches long. Take 3 strips and braid them together. Place on a greased baking sheet. Braid the remaining 3 strips and place about 6 inches away from the other loaf.

Cover the loaves and let rise until doubled in bulk, about 1 1/2 hours. Brush with the egg white and water; sprinkle with sesame seeds. Bake at 375 degrees for 35 to 40 minutes, or until the loaves sound hollow when tapped top and bottom and have a nice golden brown color. Makes 2 loaves.

—GLACIER BAY COUNTRY INN,
GUSTAVUS

PEARSON'S POND HAM BREAD

2 C. water

1 T. sugar

2 pkgs. dry yeast

2 T. salt

4 1/2 C. (about) flour

1 to 2 lbs. of cooked turkey ham
   or regular ham, ground or
   finely chopped

1 egg white

In a medium-large mixing bowl combine water, sugar, and yeast. After the yeast has softened, stir in salt. Beat in 4 cups of flour, one cup at a time. Add 1/2 cup more flour to knead by machine or hand. Add more flour if needed.

Knead firmly and thoroughly until smooth. Form into ball and place in clean, warm bowl. Cover with damp towel; let rise till about doubled in bulk.

Punch dough down lightly and divide into 4 roughly equal parts. Let rest 10 minutes. Roll each on a lightly floured surface to a 10- x 18-inch rectangle. Begin rolling the rectangle of dough from the wide side, sealing (by pressing) the roll against the rectangle with each half roll. After the first full roll, sprinkle a few tablespoons of ground ham along the sealed edge, roll over and seal again. Repeat until the entire rectangle has been rolled. Seal the edges and the final edge well. Place seam side down on lightly greased, long baking sheet which has been sprinkled with cornmeal. Repeat with remaining 3 pieces of dough. Make several shallow diagonal slashes on top of each roll. Lightly beat egg white with 1 tablespoon water; brush half over tops of rolls. Let rise until doubled in bulk.

Bake at 365 degrees for 20 minutes. Brush with remaining egg white mixture. Bake another 15 to 20 minutes. Cool on racks.

**—PEARSON'S POND B & B,
JUNEAU**

No Knead Golden Loaf Bread

1 1/2 C. warm water

1 pkg. dry yeast

1/3 C. wheat germ

1 egg

1/2 C. oatmeal

1 T. sugar

1 T. shortening

1 t. salt

4 C. flour

Combine all ingredients in bowl or food processor, mixing well until dough forms a ball. Place in a greased bowl and cover. Let rise until double in bulk. Punch down. Make loaf and put in greased bread pan. Let rise then bake at 400 degrees for 45 minutes.

**—WALLIN'S HILLTOP B & B,
ANCHOR POINT**

CHAPTER 3

Something Old,
Something New

SOURDOUGH STARTERS

Sourdough is a personal thing here in Alaska. Everyone has their own opinion about its age and aroma, and how a starter should be made. Some people are actually quite snooty about it and feel the starter should be handed down from generation to generation and that it should have a sharp, sour smell. Others are quite happy with the starter they made last night that has a milder, sweeter smell.

However you feel about the stuff, there are some general guidelines for the care and feeding of a sourdough starter. If observed, you and your starter can have a long, satisfying relationship.

For those not fortunate enough to have been given a sourdough starter by great aunt Matilda from Nome, Valdez or San Francisco, there are two commonly accepted ways to make your own (recipes follow). The starter used at Riversong Lodge uses flour, water and yeast. The other recipe, from *The Joy of Cooking*,

calls for milk, flour and sugar. The milk/sugar recipe, without added yeast, works best in kitchens where a lot of baking goes on and yeast spores in the air are prevalent.

Whichever starter recipe you choose, the best way to keep it alive and kicking is to stir it once in awhile and use it often.

To use your sourdough, remove the starter from the refrigerator the night before and check your recipe. If the recipe calls for 2 cups of starter, stir enough flour and water (or milk) into your starter to make 2 additional cups. If the recipe requires 6 cups of starter, you want to add enough flour and liquid to make 6 additional cups. Equal quantities of flour and water or milk work well, but I like a thicker batter so I add a little less liquid. Leave the starter on the counter overnight.

The next morning, your starter should be bubbling along nicely, and you can take out 2 cups of it (or whatever your recipe calls for) and refrigerate the rest.

One of the mistakes I have made (more frequently than I like to admit) is to forget to put any starter back in the refrigerator, and instead, add all of it to my recipe. Panic ensues when I discover we've just *eaten* the starter I've been feeding so carefully for months and that great aunt Sophie (Matilda's sister) kept alive for nearly 80 years. Personally, I'd be willing to bet great aunt Sophie ate her starter a time or two herself, and just whipped up a new batch without telling anyone. Or maybe she went and begged some off aunt Matilda.

—CASS CRANDALL

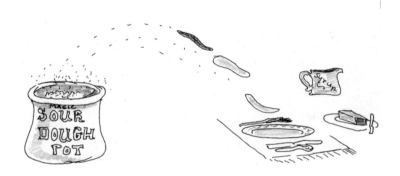

SOURDOUGH STARTER 1

1 pkg. (1 T.) dry yeast

2 C. flour

1 1/2 C. warm water

Combine all ingredients in a 2-quart pitcher. Stir it up but don't worry about getting all the lumps out. Cover the container with a lid, making sure the lid has an open spout to allow air to circulate. Remember—yeast are living organisms! Set the pitcher in a warm (85 degrees), draft-free spot. If the starter happens to bubble over, quickly clean it up: it can make a gluey mess. Keep the starter warm for 3 to 5 days, stirring once or twice a day. You should begin to smell the yeast fermenting.

Store starter in the refrigerator, but return it to room temperature before using. If you aren't using your starter frequently, stir it once a week and replenish it by adding 1 cup of water and 1 cup of flour after each use.

**—RIVERSONG LODGE,
YENTNA RIVER**

SOURDOUGH STARTER 2

1 C. lukewarm milk

1 C. flour

1/2 C. sugar

Mix ingredients well and pour into jar or crock. Cover **loosely** and let stand for 4 to 7 days, stirring daily. When starter bubbles and smells sour, use immediately or refrigerate. Stir and replenish starter as described in recipe above.

—*JOY OF COOKING* (1975)

SOURDOUGH RECIPES

CHERRY SOURDOUGH SWIRLS

1 C. sourdough starter

1/2 C. margarine

1/2 C. water

3/4 C. milk

1/2 C. sugar

1 1/2 t. salt

1 pkg. dry yeast

3 to 4 C. flour

1 can cherry pie filling

Frosting:

1 C. powdered sugar

1 t. vanilla

1 T. milk

Measure sourdough starter into bowl. Add margarine, water and milk, heated to lukewarm. Stir in sugar, salt and yeast. Gradually add enough flour to make a soft dough. Turn out onto floured surface and knead until smooth. Place dough in a greased bowl, cover with plastic wrap and refrigerate 2 hours or overnight.

Turn dough onto lightly floured surface. Divide into 18 sections. Gently roll each piece to make a 15-inch long strand. Shape on greased baking sheet by holding one end of strand in place and winding around loosely to form a coil. Tuck end firmly underneath. Place 2 inches apart and cover with cloth. Set in a warm place free from drafts and let rise 1 hour.

Make an indentation about 1 inch wide in center of each coil, pressing to bottom. Fill with cherry pie filling. Bake at 400 degrees for 12 to 15 minutes. Remove and cool on wire rack. Makes 18 rolls.

Frosting: Combine powdered sugar, vanilla, and milk. Stir until smooth and drizzle over cooled rolls.

—**BIORKA B & B,**
SITKA

SOURDOUGH COFFEE CAKE

2 C. sourdough starter

2 eggs

1/2 C. oil

1 C. sugar

2 C. flour

1/2 t. cinnamon

1/2 t. baking soda

2 t. baking powder

Topping:

1 T. flour

1/2 C. brown sugar

1/2 C. melted butter

Glaze:

1/4 C. butter

1/4 C. brown sugar

1/8 C. milk

Stir together starter, eggs and oil; add sugar and mix well. Mix flour, cinnamon, baking soda and baking powder and combine with the starter mixture. Pour batter into greased and floured 9- x 13-inch pan.

Topping: Mix ingredients and pour over batter. Swirl through batter deeply with a fork. Bake at 350 degrees for 35 to 40 minutes.

Glaze: Combine ingredients in a small saucepan and bring to a boil. Pour glaze over warm cake.

—ARCTIC TERN B & B,
SOLDOTNA

LILAC HOUSE SUMMER SOURDOUGH WAFFLES

1 C. sourdough starter

2 C. flour

2 C. milk

1 t. salt

2 t. baking soda

2 eggs

3 T. light vegetable oil

1 T. sugar

unsalted butter, melted

fresh peaches

fresh blueberries

pure maple syrup

creme fraiche, room temperature

(see p. 185)

cinnamon

Twelve hours before serving, mix starter, flour, milk and salt. Let stand in a cheesecloth-covered bowl in a warm (by Alaskan standards—70 degrees) place. Just before cooking, add soda, eggs, oil and sugar. Mix well and cook on well buttered waffle iron.

Place cooked, crisp waffles on warm plates. Pour on melted butter, then pile sliced peaches and fresh blueberries on top. Drizzle with warm maple syrup. Top with creme fraiche and sprinkle lightly with cinnamon. Serves 4.

—THE LILAC HOUSE B & B,
ANCHORAGE

SOURDOUGH SCONES

2 C. sourdough starter

3 T. butter, melted

1/2 C. flour

1/4 C. sugar

3/4 t. salt

1/2 t. soda

3 T. currants

Stir melted butter into starter. Add remaining ingredients and mix well. Knead the dough until smooth, adding more flour if necessary. Roll about 3/4-inch thick and cut into 3-inch squares. Place in a thickly buttered pan and spread additional melted butter over the tops. Let rise for about an hour, then bake at 375 degrees for 35 minutes.

—GUSTAVUS INN B & B,
GUSTAVUS

MCKINLEY/DENALI CABINS SOURDOUGH PANCAKES

2 C. sourdough starter

2 C. flour

2 C. water

2 t. oil

3 T. sugar

1/2 t. baking soda

1/4 C. hot water

Prepare starter the night before by adding flour and 2 cups water to original starter. Let sit out overnight covered with plastic wrap. Next morning, remove 2 cups of the starter and combine with the oil and sugar. (Put remaining starter back into refrigerator.) Dissolve baking soda in hot water; add to starter mixture. Cook pancakes on hot, oiled griddle.

—McKINLEY/DENALI CABINS &
BREAKFAST, DENALI PARK

POLLEN'S SOURDOUGH PANCAKES AND WAFFLES

1 C. sourdough starter

1 egg

2 T. vegetable oil

1/4 C. dry milk powder

2 T. sugar

1 t. salt

1 t. baking soda

1/4 t. cloves (optional)

1/4 t. cinnamon (optional)

The night before, mix 1 cup starter with 2 cups warm water and 2 cups white flour. Let it sit out overnight, covered. The next morning, remove 1 cup of the starter and refrigerate. This is your new starter.

To the remaining starter, add egg, oil and dry milk. Mix remaining ingredients in a small bowl then stir into batter. Mix well and let rest for a few minutes. Cook on hot griddle or waffle iron and serve with warm syrup. Blueberries may be used in place of the spices.

**—POLLEN'S B & B,
PALMER**

SOURDOUGH WAFFLES

2 C. sourdough starter

1 egg

2 t. sugar

1 t. soda

1 t. salt

*1/2 C. bran or wheat germ
  (optional)*

1 T. oil

Combine all ingredients and cook on a hot greased waffle iron.

**—LISIANSKI LODGE B & B,
PELICAN**

SOURDOUGH CINNAMON ROLLS

1/2 C. milk

1 pkg. yeast

2 T. warm water

2 C. sourdough starter (see note)

1/4 C. brown sugar

1/4 C. margarine

1 1/2 t. salt

1 egg, slightly beaten

1 1/2 C. raisins

1/2 C. walnuts or pecans

2 t. cinnamon

1/2 t. nutmeg

4 to 5 C. flour

margarine

brown sugar

cinnamon

Scald milk; set aside to cool. Sprinkle yeast over water. Set aside to soften. In large bowl combine starter, milk, yeast mixture, 1/4 cup sugar, 1/4 cup margarine, salt, egg, raisins and nuts. Set aside. In small bowl stir cinnamon, nutmeg and 1 cup flour. Beat into sourdough mix. Stir in additional flour to make a medium stiff dough. Knead 8 to 10 minutes. Cover and let rise until double in bulk. Punch down.

Divide dough in half, roll out and brush with margarine. Sprinkle with brown sugar and cinnamon to taste. Roll up jelly-roll fashion; cut each roll into 12 slices. Place slices cut side down on cookie sheets. Bake about 25 to 30 minutes at 350 degrees. Makes 24.

Note: Bear Creek B & B uses an "instant" starter made from 2 cups warm water, 2 cups flour and 1 envelope yeast. Let stand overnight or at least 6 hours.

**—BEAR CREEK B & B,
HOMER**

SOURDOUGH BISCUIT ROLLS

4 C. flour

4 C. whole wheat flour

1/2 C. sugar

6 t. baking powder

1/2 t. salt

1 C. oil

2 C. buttermilk

6 C. sourdough starter

Blend dry ingredients, then add oil, buttermilk and starter. Mix with spoon and turn out onto floured board. Knead gently 6 to 8 times until smooth. Pat gently, but do not roll. Cut with drinking glass rim, dip in melted butter and place on ungreased baking sheet. Bake at 425 degrees for 20 minutes. Makes 36.

—ILIASKA LODGE,
ILIAMNA LAKE

SOURDOUGH CORN BREAD

1/2 C. butter, melted

1 t. salt

2 C. milk

3 T. sugar

2 C. coarse ground cornmeal

2 C. sourdough starter

2 eggs

2 t. baking powder

Stir together butter, salt, milk, sugar and cornmeal in a medium-sized bowl. Stir in starter, eggs and baking powder.

Pour into a 10- x 13-inch pan and bake at 425 degrees for 40 minutes.

—ILIASKA LODGE,
ILIAMNA LAKE

SOURDOUGH MUFFINS

2 C. sourdough starter

1/3 C. sugar

1 egg

1 C. raisins

1 1/2 C. flour (about)

1 t. soda

Mix starter with sugar, egg, raisins and half the flour. Add the soda dissolved in a little water with the rest of the flour. Fold into batter until just mixed and spoon immediately into greased muffin tins. Bake at 375 degrees 10 to 15 minutes or until golden brown.

—GUSTAVUS INN BED AND
BREAKFAST, GUSTAVUS

SOURDOUGH OATMEAL MUFFINS

1 1/2 C. flour

1/2 C. brown sugar

1 C. uncooked oatmeal

1 t. salt

1 t. soda

1 egg

1/2 C. oil

1/2 C. buttermilk

3/4 C. sourdough starter

raisins, dates or nuts (optional)

Mix dry ingredients, make a well and add remaining ingredients. Mix just to moisten. Spoon into greased and floured muffin tins and bake at 350 degrees for 18 to 20 minutes. Makes 12 muffins.

—BEAVER BEND B & B,
FAIRBANKS

Iliaska Sourdough Pancakes

2 C. sourdough starter

2 T. sugar

1 egg

1/2 t. salt

4 T. oil

1 t. baking soda dissolved in 1

   T. lukewarm water

Mix sugar, egg, salt, and oil into the starter. Mix well. Add soda and water to batter just before making pancakes. Do not overmix. Batter will almost double when the soda is added. Bake on hot griddle until golden brown. Serves 4 to 6.

**—ILIASKA LODGE,
ILIAMNA LAKE**

Wright's Sourdough Pancakes

1 C. sourdough starter

1 C. milk

1 egg

3 T. oil

1 1/4 C. flour

1 t. baking powder

1/4 t. soda

1 T. sugar

Mix just before cooking and serving. Serve with reindeer sausage, real maple syrup or fruit syrup.

**—WRIGHT'S B & B,
ANCHORAGE**

—CHAPTER 4—

Time Out
for Breakfast

BREAKFAST SPECIALS

BLUEBERRY LODGE OATS

8 C. old fashioned oats

1/2 C. raisins

1/2 C. dates, chopped

1/2 C. walnuts, chopped

1/2 C. wheat germ or oat bran

apple juice

grated fresh apple

Mix first 5 ingredients and store in a covered container. To serve, half-fill individual bowls with mixture; add apple juice to almost cover. Let stand about 10 minutes. Add 1/3 cup grated apple to each bowl. Stir thoroughly and serve. Pass brown sugar, milk and yogurt.

—BLUEBERRY LODGE B & B,
JUNEAU

PILOT LIGHT YOGURT

1 qt. milk (see note)

2 T. plain yogurt

Note: Milk from our Nubian goats makes great yogurt, but cow's milk may be substituted.

Heat milk in saucepan to 180 degrees. Let cool to about 105 degrees (will feel hot but not burn you). Mix small amount of warm milk with plain yogurt until rather smooth. Pour milk into warmed quart jar. Stir in milk-yogurt mixture. Preheat oven to just over 100 degrees and turn off. Put jar in oven overnight with pilot light to keep it warm. The next morning refrigerate the yogurt. (For those without gas ovens, to keep yogurt at about 104 degrees overnight.) Use yogurt to make salad dressings, on sandwiches or baked potatoes, or whip with fruit in blender.

—TIMBERLINGS B & B,
PALMER

EGG DISHES

ALASKAN BRUNCH

6 to 7 slices bread, cubed

1 lb. sausage or ham, precooked

1/2 lb. old English cheese, grated

3 eggs, beaten

1/2 t. dry mustard

2 C. milk

1/2 t. salt

1/2 C. butter, melted

Mix bread, sausage or ham and cheese in 9- by 13-inch pan. Mix eggs, mustard, milk and salt; pour over bread mixture. Pour melted butter over all. Cover; refrigerate overnight. Uncover and bake at 325 degrees for 1 hour. Serves 12.

—EAGLES' REST B & B,
PALMER

SUMMER INN EGG CASSEROLE

16 slices bread (crusts removed),
   cut into cubes

1 lb. ham, cubed

1 lb. Cheddar cheese, grated

1 1/2 C. Swiss cheese, cubed

6 eggs

3 C. milk

1/2 t. onion salt

1/2 t. dry mustard

3 C. cornflakes, crushed

1/2 C. melted butter

Spread half of bread in bottom of a greased 9- x 13-inch pan. Add ham and both cheeses. Cover with remaining bread. Mix eggs, milk, onion salt and dry mustard. Pour over bread, cover and refrigerate overnight.

Before baking, mix cornflakes and melted butter; sprinkle on top. Bake uncovered at 375 degrees for 50 to 60 minutes or until no longer runny.

—THE SUMMER INN B & B,
HAINES

THE LOST CHORD BREAKFAST CASSEROLE

5 slices bread, torn into pieces

2 C. Cheddar cheese, grated

4 eggs, beaten

3/4 t. mustard

2 1/4 C. milk

1 1/2 lbs. ham, finely chopped

1 C. condensed cream of
  mushroom soup

3/4 C. milk

Place bread in bottom of a 9- by 13-inch baking dish; top with cheese. Mix eggs, mustard and milk. Pour over bread and cheese. Sprinkle ham on top. Refrigerate overnight. In the morning, combine mushroom soup with milk. Pour over casserole. Bake at 300 degrees for 1 hour.

—THE LOST CHORD B & B,
JUNEAU

MUSHROOM SOUFFLE

2 eggs

2 T. butter

1/4 C. green onions

1 C. mushrooms, sliced

1 C. ham, chopped

2 T. butter

2 T. flour

2 C. milk

2 C. sharp Cheddar cheese,
  shredded

seasoned bread crumbs

Partially scramble eggs, set aside. Saute next 4 ingredients and set aside. Combine butter and flour in saucepan; stir over low heat for 1 minute then add milk and cook until mixture thickens. Add cheese, stirring until it melts. Mix eggs, onion-mushroom mixture and cheese sauce and pour into 9- by 13-inch greased baking pan. Top with seasoned bread crumbs and bake at 350 degrees for 30 minutes.

—KARRAS B & B,
SITKA

PINEAPPLE BRUNCH CASSEROLE

1 C. biscuit mix

1 C. milk

4 eggs, lightly beaten

6 T. butter, melted

1 t. Dijon mustard

onion powder (to taste; optional)

nutmeg (to taste; optional)

1/2 t. cooked ham, diced

1 C. Cheddar cheese, shredded

2 green onions, chopped

1 8-oz. can crushed pineapple

Drain pineapple. Combine biscuit mix, milk, eggs, butter, mustard, onion powder and nutmeg in mixing bowl until smooth. Stir in ham, cheese, onions and pineapple. Pour into greased 9-inch pie pan. Bake at 350 degrees 35 to 40 minutes or until set. Serves 6.

**—ALASKA'S 7 GABLES,
FAIRBANKS**

CHILI EGG PUFF

10 eggs

1 t. baking powder

2 C. cottage cheese

1 4-oz. can diced chilies

1/2 C. flour

1/2 t. salt

1/2 C. margarine, melted

1 lb. jack cheese, grated

Mix ingredients in order given. Pour into greased 9- by 13-inch pan. Bake at 350 degrees for 30 minutes or until knife comes out clean. (Can be mixed the night before and refrigerated.)

**—PAT'S PLACE B & B,
WASILLA**

BRIE OMELETTE

4 green onions, thinly sliced

2 T. unsalted butter

5 large eggs

1/2 t. dried dill, chopped

1/2 t. dried thyme

3 T. sour cream

3 oz. Brie cheese, sliced

If possible, use a well seasoned 5- or 6-inch iron skillet. Saute onion in 2 tablespoons butter until limp, being careful not to burn. Beat eggs, herbs and sour cream together with a wire whisk until very frothy. Pour into the iron skillet with the cooked onions and butter and cook over medium heat. As the omelette cooks on the bottom, take a fork and gently lift the cooked egg to the surface (this keeps the egg from getting too brown). When approximately half cooked, place 1/4-inch slices of Brie on top. Cover with a tight-fitting lid and continue to cook until Brie is very soft but eggs are still slightly runny on top. Fold omelette in half. Serve with hot croissants, butter, jam and fresh strawberries. Serves 2.

**—THE LILAC HOUSE B & B,
ANCHORAGE**

CRAB BRUNCH SCRAMBLE

6 to 8 oz. crabmeat, fresh or
   frozen

1/4 C. butter

2 T. sliced green onion

8 eggs, slightly beaten

1/2 C. sour cream

2 T. Parmesan cheese

1/8 t. salt

3 English muffins, split, toasted
   and buttered

Defrost and drain crab if frozen. Break into bite-sized pieces. In a medium skillet, melt butter, add green onion and saute over medium heat 1 to 2 minutes. Beat together eggs, sour cream, cheese and salt. Add egg mixture and crab to green onion in skillet. Cook, stirring constantly, until done. Serve eggs over toasted muffin halves. Makes 3 to 6 servings.

—CLAY'S QUALITY B & B,
HOMER

FRANK'S CAN'T-FAIL CRUSTLESS BREAKFAST QUICHE

2 C. large curd cottage cheese

4 C. extra sharp cheese,
   shredded

1 C. broccoli, potatoes or ham,
   chopped

10 large eggs

1 C. milk

Combine all ingredients and pour into 9- x 12-inch oiled baking dish. Bake at 350 degrees 1 hour. May be frozen then microwaved or reheated conventionally.

Variation: Frank's favorite variation is to add 1/4 teaspoon of dried Jalapeno peppers.

—ALL THE COMFORTS OF
HOME B & B, ANCHORAGE

IMPOSSIBLE BACON PIE

12 slices bacon, fried crisp

1 C. natural Swiss cheese

1/3 C. onion, chopped

1 C. Bisquick

2 C. milk

4 eggs

1/4 t. pepper

Grease a 10-inch quiche dish or pie pan.

Sprinkle bacon, cheese and onion in pan. Beat remaining ingredients until smooth; 15 seconds in blender on high or 1 minute with a hand beater. Pour into pan and bake at 400 degrees until knife inserted between center and edge comes out clean, 35 to 40 minutes. Cool 5 minutes before serving.

**—EDE DEN B & B,
WASILLA**

KRUGER SCRAMBLER

2 T. butter

3 oz. cream cheese, softened

3 eggs

1/2 C. shallots, finely chopped

1/3 C. whipping cream

Spray a large skillet liberally with nonstick cooking spray and set on low heat. Add butter and cream cheese and heat slowly.

In a bowl, beat eggs with shallots and cream. Add to skillet and cook until eggs are softly set. Transfer to warm plates. Salt and pepper to taste.

**—ALL THE COMFORTS OF
HOME, ANCHORAGE**

MAKE-AHEAD EGGS BENEDICT

4 English muffins, split & toasted

16 thin slices Canadian bacon

8 eggs

Sauce:

1/4 C. margarine

1/4 C. all purpose flour

1 t. paprika

1/8 t. ground nutmeg

1/8 t. pepper

2 C. milk

2 C. Swiss cheese, shredded

1/2 C. dry white wine (optional)

1/2 C. cornflakes, crushed

1 T. margarine, melted

In 9 x 13 inch glass baking pan arrange muffins, cut side up. Place 2 bacon slices on each muffin half. Half fill 10-inch skillet with water and bring just to boiling. Break 1 egg into a dish. Carefully slide egg into water. Repeat with 3 more eggs. Simmer, uncovered, 3 minutes or until just set. Remove eggs with a slotted spoon. Repeat with remaining eggs. Place 1 egg on top of each muffin stack.

Sauce: In a medium pan melt 1/4 cup margarine. Stir in flour, paprika, nutmeg and pepper. Add milk all at once. Cook and stir until thickened and bubbly. Add cheese and stir until melted. Stir in wine. Carefully spoon over muffin stacks. Cover; chill overnight. Before serving, top with cornflake crumbs and drizzle with melted margarine. Bake, uncovered, at 375 degrees for 20 to 25 minutes or until heated through. Serves 8.

**THE SUMMER INN B & B,
HAINES**

POTATO-BACON OMELET

6 slices bacon

1 C. potatoes, pared and diced

2 T. onion, chopped

1/2 t. salt

1 T. dry parsley

1 T. cooking oil

8 eggs, well beaten

1 T. water

1/4 t. salt

1/8 t. pepper

In a small skillet, fry bacon until crisp. Remove and drain on paper towels. Crumble. Pour off all but 2 tablespoons of the bacon fat; add potato, onion and 1/2 teaspoon salt. Cook until potatoes are tender and golden. Stir in parsley and bacon. Set aside. Heat oil in a 10-inch skillet over medium heat. Beat together eggs, water, 1/4 teaspoon salt and pepper. Stir in potato mixture and pour into skillet. With fork, lift cooked edges so that uncooked portion flows underneath. Slide pan back and forth to avoid sticking. Cook until mixture is set, but top still moist. Fold in half and slide onto a warm platter.

—ARCTIC TERN B & B,
SOLDOTNA

POTATO, ONION AND CHEESE FRITTATA

3 potatoes, diced

1 T. oil

1/4 C. onion, diced

6 eggs

1 C. milk

2 T. butter, melted

1/2 t. salt

1/2 t. pepper

4 oz. Cheddar cheese, shredded

In a large frying pan, brown diced potato in oil for 10 minutes. Add onion and brown two more minutes, and set aside. In a bowl, whisk the eggs, milk, melted butter, salt and pepper. If using a cast iron skillet, simply pour egg mixture over cooked potatoes. Otherwise, transfer the cooked potatoes to a greased 9- x 9-inch baking pan. Sprinkle cheese on top. Bake at 400 degrees for 20 minutes or until set and brown. Serves 6 to 8.

Variation: Sprinkle crumbled bacon over the top.

—BLUEBERRY LODGE B & B, JUNEAU

SCOTTISH EGGS

6 eggs, hard cooked and chilled

12 oz. Jimmy Dean pork sausage

1/4 C. flour

2 beaten eggs

3/4 C. cornflake crumbs

Form sausage into 6 patties. Wrap 1 patty around each hard cooked egg. Roll in flour, beaten egg and then crumbs. Bake at 400 degrees for 20 minutes.

—DAYBREAK B & B, FAIRBANKS

Skillet Egg Breakfast Dish

1 C. ham or sausage, chopped
   (can use leftovers)

1/2 C. green pepper, chopped

3 to 4 potatoes, cooked and
   diced

1/2 C. chopped onion

1 T. oil

6 eggs, well beaten

1 C. shredded jack or Cheddar
   cheese

Saute ham or sausage, green pepper, potatoes and onions in oil. Pour eggs over mixture and cook, stirring constantly, until eggs are done. Remove from heat and top with shredded cheese. Serve when cheese is melted. Serves 4.

**—MARLOW'S KENAI RIVER
B & B, SOLDOTNA**

French Toast Casserole

1 large loaf French bread

1 1/2 C. milk

6 large eggs

1 C. half-and-half

1 t. vanilla

1/4 t. cinnamon

1/4 t. nutmeg

Topping:

1/4 C. butter, softened

1/2 C. brown sugar

1 T. corn syrup

Cut bread in 1 1/2-inch thick slices and place in 9- x 13-inch pan. Mix milk, eggs, half-and-half, vanilla, cinnamon and nutmeg. Beat well. Pour over bread and refrigerate overnight. Next morning, mix topping ingredients. Microwave 1 minute on low. Pour mixture over bread and bake at 350 degrees 30 to 40 minutes or until light brown. Serve warm. Makes about 6 servings.

**—ARCTIC TERN B & B,
SOLDOTNA**

STEAMBOAT OMELET

16 slices bread, crusts removed

8 slices ham

8 slices Canadian bacon

8 slices Cheddar cheese

6 eggs

1/2 t. salt

pepper to taste

1/4 t. dry mustard

1/4 C. onion, minced

1/4 C. green pepper, finely
  chopped

3 C. milk

1 to 2 t. Worcestershire sauce

1/2 C. butter, melted

1 C. crushed potato chips

In a baking pan place 8 slices of bread; stack ham, Canadian bacon and cheese on top. Mix eggs, salt, pepper, dry mustard, onion, green pepper, milk and Worcestershire sauce. Pour over stacks. Put remaining 8 slices of bread on top. Cover and refrigerate overnight.

In morning melt butter and pour over bread. Sprinkle crushed potato chips on top. Bake at 350 degrees for 1 hour or until done.

**—ARCTIC TERN B & B,
SOLDOTNA**

SOUR CREAM AND HAM OMELET

5 eggs, separated

1/2 C. sour cream

3 T. parsley, chopped

3 T. onions, chopped

1 C. cooked ham, finely diced

1 1/2 T. butter

In a bowl, beat egg yolks until very thick and lemon colored. Stir in sour cream, parsley, onions and ham. In a large bowl using clean beaters, beat egg whites until stiff, moist peaks form. Gently fold yolk mixture and whites together.

In a 10-inch frying pan with ovenproof handle, melt butter over medium heat, tilting pan to coat bottom and sides. Pour omelet mixture into pan and gently smooth surface with a spoon. Reduce heat to low and cook until edges are lightly browned, about 7 to 10 minutes. Bake at 325 degrees 12 to 15 minutes or until knife inserted in center comes out clean. Serve warm with additional sour cream. Makes 4 servings.

—ARCTIC TERN B & B,
SOLDOTNA

PANCAKES, BLINTZES, CREPES & WAFFLES

BEST OF ALL CREPES

Crepes:

2/3 C. flour

1/2 T. salt

3 eggs, beaten

1 C. milk

Filling:

2 8-oz. pkg. cream cheese

1/2 C. sugar

1 C. cottage cheese

1 T. vanilla

Topping:

1/4 C. water

1 C. sugar

2 T. cornstarch

2 C. fresh blueberries or sliced
   strawberries

Crepes: Combine flour, salt and eggs. Beat until smooth. Gradually add milk and mix well. Pour 1/4 cup of batter into hot skillet, swirling pan to coat evenly, and cook until light brown on both sides. Remove from pan and repeat until batter is gone.

Filling: Combine cream cheese with other ingredients. Mix well.

Topping: In saucepan, stir together water, sugar and cornstarch. Cook over medium heat, stirring often, until mixture thickens and boils. Remove from heat and add fruit.

Spoon filling onto center of crepe and roll up. Spoon topping over crepes and serve.

**—BEST OF ALL B & B,
VALDEZ**

HATCHER PASS BLINTZES

Pancakes:

5 eggs

3 C. milk

1 1/2 t. salt

1/3 C. oil

3 T. sugar

3 C. (about) flour

Filling:

4 C. cottage cheese

cinnamon to taste

2 C. Monterey Jack cheese,
    shredded

2 T. brown sugar

2 apples, shredded

Pancakes: Mix first 5 ingredients in a blender; add enough flour to make a thin batter. Grease skillet and pour in enough batter to thinly cover the bottom. Cook until lightly brown on the bottom, turn and cook other side. Repeat until all batter is used.

Filling: Mix ingredients in bowl. Fill pancakes and roll up. Serve with or without syrup. Makes about 12 servings.

**—HATCHER PASS B & B,
PALMER**

BETHEL BLUEBERRY BLINTZES

Crepes:

2 C. milk

4 to 6 eggs

2 C. flour

1 t. orange extract, vanilla or
  nutmeg

Filling:

2 C. whole raw almonds

8 oz. cream cheese

2 T. sugar

1 t. cinnamon

2 lbs. cottage cheese

1 t. vanilla

Topping:

4 T. cornstarch

1/2 C. sugar

4 C. blueberries

1 C. water

Crepes: Beat ingredients in blender until smooth. Let sit 1 hour. If sour, add a little baking soda. Stir before use. If too thick, add a little milk. Cook on hot griddle as for pancakes. (Batter keeps in refrigerator 1 week or more.)

Filling: Chop almonds fine in food processor. Add cold cream cheese and process until combined. Add remaining ingredients and process 1 to 2 minutes until mixed well.

Topping: Mix cornstarch and sugar. Sprinkle over blueberries in large microwave dish. Add water and stir. Microwave on high, stirring every 3 to 4 minutes until boiling.

Fill crepes, roll up and pour topping over. Warm in 325 degree oven. Garnish with sour cream. Serves 10 to 12.

—WILSON'S HOSTEL B & B,
BETHEL

BLUEBERRY WAFFLES

3 C. flour

1 C. oat bran

1/4 C. wheat germ or rice bran

1/2 t. salt

1 t. baking powder

1/3 C. oil

2 eggs, beaten

3 C. milk

1 C. blueberries (fresh or frozen)

Stir first 7 ingredients in large bowl until crumbly. Add milk slowly while stirring. Do not overmix. Add blueberries and mix gently.

Cook in waffle iron until light brown.

—BLUEBERRY LODGE B & B, JUNEAU

PUFF PANCAKES

6 T. butter

1 C. milk

2/3 C. flour

1/2 t. nutmeg or cardamom

1/2 t. salt

2 eggs

2 T. sugar

Melt half of butter in each of 2 pie pans. Mix remaining ingredients in blender. Pour half in each pie pan. Bake at 400 degrees about 20 minutes. Pancakes will puff up, but be soft in the center. Serve immediately with berry sauces or cinnamon sugar. Serves 2.

—TIMBERLINGS B & B, PALMER

FLUFFY PANCAKE

1 C. flour

4 large eggs

1 C. milk

8 T. butter

4 T. powdered sugar

pinch of nutmeg

juice of half a lemon

Mix the first three ingredients (blender works well). Leave the mixture a little lumpy. Melt butter in a 9- x 13-inch glass pan. Pour in the batter. Bake at 350 degrees until golden, 15 to 20 minutes. Sprinkle with powdered sugar and a pinch of nutmeg. Return briefly to oven. Sprinkle with lemon juice. Serve with syrup or fruit sauce.

**—HATCHER PASS B & B,
PALMER**

BAKED HAWAIIAN PANCAKE

3 eggs

pinch of salt

3/4 C. flour

1/2 t. vanilla or lemon extract

3/4 C. milk

1 1/2 T. butter

Combine first 5 ingredients, beat until smooth and set aside. Melt butter in ovenproof skillet; when quite hot, pour in batter. Bake at 450 degrees for 10 minutes. This will puff up when done. Remove from oven and immediately ladle on chopped fruit of any kind; the more varied the fruit, the better! Cut into wedges to serve.

**—PACIFICA GUEST HOUSE,
BETHEL**

FRUIT CREPE STRUDELS

Crepes:

1 C. flour

2 eggs

1 1/2 C. milk

1 T. oil

Filling:

1 20-oz. can fruit pie filling

1/2 C. nuts, finely chopped and
toasted

1/2 t. lemon peel, grated

1/2 t. vanilla

For assembly:

1/2 C. butter or margarine,
melted

6 T. fine dry bread crumbs

1 T. sugar

1/4 t. ground cinnamon

Crepes: Combine ingredients in bowl and beat with rotary beater until blended. Heat a lightly greased 10-inch skillet; pour in 1/3 cup batter and tilt skillet to spread evenly. Cook, browning only one side, until done. Repeat until all batter is used

Filling: Stir ingredients together in small bowl and set aside.

Brush the unbrowned side of each crepe with 1 tablespoon melted butter; sprinkle with 1 tablespoon bread crumbs. Spoon a scant 1/4 cup filling in middle of each crepe and roll up. Place rolled crepes seam side down on lightly greased baking sheet. Brush with remaining melted butter. Combine sugar and cinnamon; sprinkle on top. Bake at 400 degrees until crispy, about 15 minutes. Cut in pieces. Serves 12.

**—ALASKA'S 7 GABLES B & B,
FAIRBANKS**

PEACHY PECAN CREPES

Crepes:

1 C. flour

1 1/2 C. milk

2 eggs

1 T. oil

1/2 t. salt

Filling:

6 oz. cream cheese

3 T. sugar

2 T. milk

1/2 t. grated orange peel

1/4 t. vanilla

1/2 C. pecans, chopped

Sauce:

1 29-oz. can sliced peaches

2 T. cornstarch

1/2 C. orange juice

2 T. lemon juice

2 T. butter

Crepes: Blend flour, milk, eggs, oil and salt, beating until well blended. Heat a lightly greased 6-inch skillet. Spoon in 2 tablespoons batter, tilting to spread over bottom of pan. Brown both sides lightly. Remove from pan and transfer to plate, placing wax paper between crepes. Repeat until all batter is used.

Filling: Blend cream cheese, sugar, milk, orange peel and vanilla. Reserve chopped pecans for assembly.

Sauce: Drain peaches; reserve syrup. In chafing dish or skillet mix syrup into cornstarch. Add orange juice, lemon juice, and butter. Cook and stir until thickened and bubbly, then add peaches.

To assemble, spoon filling in center of crepe; sprinkle with chopped pecans. Fold in half, then in half again, forming a triangle. Repeat with remaining crepes. Add crepes to sauce and heat through. (Crepes can be assembled the night before and heated in the oven the next morning.)

—ALASKA'S SEVEN GABLES
B & B, FAIRBANKS

MAGIC CANYON DELIGHT

2 T. dry yeast

1/2 C. warm water

1 t. sugar

1 egg

2 1/2 C. flour

1/2 t. salt

3/4 C. margarine or shortening

8 oz. cream cheese, room
   temperature

1/2 C. sour cream

2 T. lemon juice

1 egg beaten with 1 T. water

Strawberries (for topping)

Mix yeast, water and sugar; let stand 10 minutes. Add egg. Cut margarine into flour and salt. Add yeast mixture and stir to form a dough. Roll between waxed paper into a large rectangle. Remove paper and place dough on baking sheet.

Mix cream cheese, sour cream and lemon juice and spread over half of crust; fold crust over and seal edges. Brush with egg wash. Bake for 30 minutes at 375 degrees. Top with sliced strawberries and serve.

—**MAGIC CANYON RANCH
B & B, HOMER**

D. Tillion

FRENCH TOAST

ORANGE FRENCH TOAST

2 eggs

1/2 C. orange juice

1 t. brown sugar

5 to 6 slices French bread, cut
  into 3/4-inch slices

maple syrup

In a pie plate, combine eggs, orange juice and brown sugar. Beat well with fork. Dip bread into egg mixture, turning to coat both sides and letting stand 30 seconds per side until thoroughly soaked. In a skillet or on a griddle, cook bread on both sides in oil over medium heat for 2 to 3 minutes on each side or until golden brown. Serve with syrup.

**—ARCTIC TERN B & B,
SOLDOTNA**

CRUNCHY CRUST FRENCH TOAST

1 egg

1/3 C. milk

2 t. sugar

ground cinnamon

1/2 C. flaked coconut

1/3 C. corn flakes, crushed

4 slices white bread

3 T. margarine

Blend egg, milk, sugar and a few shakes of cinnamon. Mix coconut and corn flakes. Dip bread slices in egg mixture, then coat with coconut mixture. Heat margarine in a skillet over medium heat. Cook prepared bread slices in skillet until light golden on both sides. Serve with additional margarine and maple syrup.

**—WINDSOCK INN B & B,
DOUGLAS**

PUFFIN'S FRENCH TOAST

2 eggs

2 C. milk

1 t. cinnamon

1/2 t. nutmeg

Sourdough bread, sliced

powdered sugar

Mix first 4 ingredients. Dip bread slices on both sides. Fry in margarine until light brown, then microwave 1 minute, or until done. Sift powdered sugar over French toast before serving.

—PUFFIN'S B & B,
GUSTAVUS

VERY FRENCH TOAST

4 croissants, day old

6 large eggs

6 T. cream

1 T. orange rind, grated

4 T. Grand Marnier liqueur

6 T. unsalted butter

powdered sugar (garnish)

strawberries (garnish)

orange slices (garnish)

creme fraiche (see recipe, p. 185)

melted butter

maple syrup

Split croissants lengthwise and set aside. Beat eggs, cream, orange rind and Grand Marnier with a wire whisk until slightly frothy. Heat heavy skillet and melt 3 tablespoons butter. Dip croissants, half at a time, into the egg mixture. Cook croissant halves in butter in medium hot skillet. Turn when slightly brown. Continue cooking until all are cooked, adding more butter if needed. Sprinkle with powdered sugar and garnish with strawberries and orange slices. Pass creme fraiche, butter and maple syrup. Serves 4.

—THE LILAC HOUSE B & B,
ANCHORAGE

STUFFED FRENCH TOAST

8 oz. ricotta cheese

1 t. vanilla

1 T. brown sugar

1/2 C. walnuts, chopped

1 loaf of French or Italian bread

(not a baguette)

4 eggs

1 C. milk

pinch of nutmeg

In food processor using the steel blade or in blender, mix ricotta, vanilla, and brown sugar until light. Add nuts and process lightly just until mixed.

Cut bread into slices 1 1/2 to 2 inches thick. Cut a horizontal slit in the side of each slice, forming a pocket. Spoon 1 or 2 tablespoons of filling into each pocket.

Mix eggs, milk and nutmeg. Carefully dip both sides of stuffed bread slices into egg-milk mixture until bread is just moistened. (If bread gets too wet, stuffing will come out.)

Cook on lightly greased griddle or skillet until 1 side is brown, about 5 minutes; turn and brown other side. (Or, bake in long, flat pan at 400 degrees about 10 minutes on each side or until golden.) Serves 8 to 10.

—WASILLA LAKE B & B,
WASILLA

—*CHAPTER 5*—

Soup's On!

ALL-TIME FAVORITE CHILI

2 16-oz. cans dark red kidney
  beans

2 lbs. ground beef

1 clove garlic, minced

1 1/2 lbs. onions, chopped

2 16-oz. cans whole peeled
  tomatoes

1 16-oz. can tomato sauce

1 1/2 T. chili powder

1 t. cumin

1/2 t. sugar

cheese

Drain and rinse kidney beans. Cook beef, garlic and onion until meat is browned. Drain off fat. Stir in tomatoes (with juice), tomato sauce, chili powder, cumin and sugar. Bring to a boil and add kidney beans. Reduce heat; stir and simmer for 20 minutes. Serve with shredded cheese and onions. Makes 8 to 10 servings.

**—ILIASKA LODGE,
ILIAMNA LAKE**

BEER CHEESE SOUP

1/2 C. butter

1/2 C. celery

1/2 C. carrot

1/2 C. onion

1/2 C. flour

1/2 t. dry mustard

5 C. chicken stock

6 oz. Cheddar cheese, grated

2 T. Parmesan-Romano cheese

1 11-oz. bottle beer

salt and pepper to taste

Cut vegetables into 1/8-inch dice. Saute in butter over low heat until done, but not browned. Blend in flour, dry mustard and chicken stock. Cook 5 minutes. Stir in Cheddar cheese, Parmesan-Romano cheese and beer. Add salt and pepper to taste. Simmer 30 minutes. Serve with French bread and salad.

—MEYERS CHUCK LODGE,
MEYERS CHUCK

GAZPACHO

1/2 C. olive oil

1/4 C. red wine vinegar

1 t. black pepper

pinch of cayenne pepper

2 large cans V-8 vegetable juice

4 cucumbers

3 garlic cloves, crushed

8 tomatoes

2 red onions

3 green peppers

Whisk oil and vinegar together. Add spices and V-8. Dice all vegetables and add to liquid. Serve chilled. Garnish with fresh parsley and sour cream if desired.

—ALL THE COMFORTS OF
HOME, ANCHORAGE

CARROT SOUP

1/2 C. butter

1/2 C. onions, chopped

1/2 C. celery, chopped

2 lbs. carrots, sliced or grated

2 C. chicken stock

water

1 t. white pepper

2 T. cumin

1/2 C. whipping cream

fresh chives, chopped

Melt butter in large saucepan. Add onions and celery; cook until tender. Add carrots, chicken stock and enough water to cover the carrots. Add seasonings and cook over medium heat until carrots are tender. Puree in blender; reheat if necessary. Ladle into soup bowls. Whip cream and put into pastry bag fitted with writing tip. Pipe thin, concentric rings of cream onto soup. Make "spider web" design using tip of knife; start at center and drag through the rings to the outside of the bowl; repeat around the bowl. Sprinkle with chives. Serves 8.

**—GLACIER BAY COUNTRY INN,
GUSTAVUS**

BOUILLABAISSE

1/4 C. olive oil

2/3 C. onion, chopped

2 leeks, chopped

1 clove garlic, crushed

2 tomatoes, chopped

1 T. parsley, minced

1/2 bay leaf

1/2 t. savory

1/2 t. fennel

1/8 t. saffron

1 1/2 t. salt

1/4 t. pepper

1 C. clam juice or 1 can stewed
  tomatoes

2 lbs. halibut, cubed

1/2 lb. shrimp

1/2 lb. crab

1/2 lb. clams

Cook onion, leeks and garlic in oil in kettle until onion is tender. Add tomatoes, herbs, spices, clam juice or stewed tomatoes and halibut cubes (liquid should barely cover). Bring rapidly to boil. Reduce heat and simmer 10 minutes or until halibut is almost done. Add shrimp, crab and clams. Cook 3 to 5 minutes longer, or until shellfish is done.

**—FAVORITE BAY INN,
ANGOON**

CHEESE SOUP

2 chicken bouillon cubes

2 C. water

3 C. chopped broccoli

1/2 C. chopped celery

1/2 C. carrots, sliced

1 T. chopped onion

3 C. milk

4 T. flour

1 t. parsley

3/4 t. salt

dash pepper

1/2 lb. Velveeta or Cheddar
  cheese, cut into cubes

Mix bouillon cubes with water. Cook broccoli, celery, carrots and onion in bouillon until tender. Put 1/2 cup of the milk in a small jar, add the flour and shake well. Stir this into the vegetables along with the remaining milk and the parsley, salt and pepper. Stir and cook over low heat until thick. Add cheese and stir until it melts. Do not boil.

—THE SUMMER INN B& B, HAINES

CLAM CHOWDER

1/2 lb. bacon, diced

3 C. onions, diced

3 C. celery, diced

4 T. dried tarragon

2 T. dried thyme

2 bay leaves

2 C. flour

1 qt. white wine

1 1/2 qt. clam juice

1 qt. milk

2 C. whipping cream

2 1/2 lbs. clams, chopped

1 1/2 lbs. potatoes, cooked and
   diced

roux to thicken (equal amounts
   of flour and butter cooked
   together briefly)

Saute bacon in large pot. Add onions and celery when bacon is brown and saute until translucent. Add herbs, simmer for 1 to 2 minutes. Add flour, stir thoroughly and cook but do not let flour brown. Add wine, clam juice, and 3 quarts of water. Bring to boil, stirring occasionally. Add milk, cream, clams and potatoes. Bring to boil, stirring to prevent scorching on bottom of pot. Add roux to desired thickness. Remove bay leaves and serve.

Note: This chowder freezes very well. To freeze, omit the whipping cream and diced potatoes. They can be added when soup is served.

**—DENALI WILDERNESS LODGE
DENALI PARK**

COUNTRY CAULIFLOWER SOUP

2 T. vegetable oil

1/2 C. onion, chopped

1 small carrot, peeled and
   grated

1 C. celery, chopped

1 head cauliflower (about 1 lb.),
   cut in flowerettes

2 T. parsley, chopped

8 C. chicken stock

1/2 t. pepper

1 t. tarragon

1 bay leaf

1/4 C. butter

3/4 C. flour

2 C. milk

1 C. half-and-half

salt

In large soup pot, heat oil, add onion and saute until translucent. Add carrot and celery and cook 2 minutes, stirring. Add cauliflower and 1 tablespoon of the parsley. Cover, reduce heat to low, and cook 15 minutes, stirring occasionally. Add chicken stock and seasonings and bring to a boil over medium heat, then reduce heat and simmer for 5 minutes. Melt butter in a medium-sized saucepan and stir in flour. Slowly add milk, whisking constantly to blend. Bring to boil over medium heat while stirring, until mixture is thick and smooth. Remove from heat and stir in the half and half. Stir this sauce into simmering soup and continue to simmer gently for 20 minutes. Just before serving, remove bay leaf, stir in remaining parsley and add salt to taste. 10 servings.

—RIVERSONG LODGE,
YENTNA RIVER

CRAB BISQUE

2 C. celery, chopped

1 C. onion, chopped

1/2 C. butter

3 C. double-strength chicken
     stock

4 C. milk

2 C. cream

1 t. white pepper

1/2 t. salt (optional)

3 T. cornstarch

3 T. water

1 1/2 lbs. crab meat

fresh chives or paprika

Saute celery and onion in butter until tender. Add chicken stock, milk, cream, pepper and salt. Bring to simmer. Dissolve cornstarch in water and stir into soup to thicken. Simmer about 2 minutes, add crab and turn off heat. (The heat of the soup will warm the crab). Garnish with fresh chives or shake paprika through a stencil onto top of soup for pretty design. Serves 8.

—GLACIER BAY COUNTRY INN, GUSTAVUS

CREAM OF BROCCOLI SOUP

1 C. butter

1 C. onions

1/2 C. green onions

1 1/2 C. celery

3 C. chicken stock

1 t. white pepper

dash of salt (optional)

10 C. broccoli, chopped

Melt butter in large saucepan. Add onions and celery; cook until tender. Add the chicken stock, seasonings, broccoli and just enough water to cover. Boil until the broccoli is just tender. Pour about 3 cups at a time into a blender and puree. Serves 8 to 12.

—GLACIER BAY COUNTRY INN, GUSTAVUS

FRENCH MARKET SOUP

3 T. dry yellow split peas

1/4 C. dry black-eyed peas

2 1/2 T. dry green split peas

1/4 C. dry pearl barley

2 1/2 T. dry pinto beans

2 1/2 T. dry pink beans or small
   red beans

2 1/2 T. dry garbanzo beans

2 1/2 T. dry lentil beans

2 1/2 T. dry lima beans

1 1/2 T. dry mung beans

1/3 C. dried black beans

1 28-oz. can plum tomatoes,
   diced

2 medium yellow onions,
   chopped

6 stalks celery, chopped

2 cloves garlic, minced

1 or 2 chicken breasts, skinned,
   boned and diced

In a stock pot, heat bean soup stock (see recipe on facing page) just to boiling (do not boil); reduce heat to simmer. Thoroughly wash and pick over peas, barley, and beans; add to stock. Add tomatoes, onions, celery and garlic; simmer, covered, 3 hours or until beans are tender. Add chicken; simmer 30 minutes, or until chicken is cooked. Makes 8 quarts.

Bean Soup Stock:

2 T. dried parsley

1 T. thyme

1 T. marjoram

2 bay leaves

2 T. celery seed

1 meaty ham hock, about 2 1/2
   to 3 lbs.

3 qts. water

1 T. salt

Bean soup stock: Measure parsley, thyme, marjoram, bay leaves and celery seed into a square of cheesecloth and tie cloth securely at the top with a string. Combine with ham hock, water and salt in a stock pot. Bring slowly to a boil, removing scum and fat as they float to the top. Cover and simmer 2 1/2 to 3 hours. (Do not boil or fat will be reabsorbed into the broth, making it cloudy.)

Refrigerate overnight. Skim and discard fat that solidifies on the top. Cut ham off bone, reserving only very lean meat. Dice and return to stock pot with seasoning pouch. Discard ham bones and ham fat. Use stock at once, or store in refrigerator or freezer for later use.

**—FAVORITE BAY INN,
ANGOON**

HAMBURGER BARLEY SOUP

1 1/2 lb. ground beef

3 beef boullion cubes

6 C. water

2 C. carrots, sliced

1 1/2 C. onion, chopped

1 1/2 C. celery, chopped

1/2 C. green pepper, chopped

1/3 C. barley

1 t. salt

dash pepper

2 bay leaves

1/4 C. catsup

1 28-oz. can tomatoes

1 8-oz. can tomato sauce

Brown meat and drain. Stir in remaining ingredients. Bring to a boil. Reduce heat, cover and simmer for 1 hour. Remove bay leaves. Serves 10

**—BEAVER BEND B & B,
FAIRBANKS**

MEXICAN MEATBALL SOUP

Meatballs:

1 lb. ground beef

1/4 C. raw rice

2 t. chili powder

1 t. salt

1/4 t. oregano leaves

1 clove garlic, minced

Soup:

1/2 C. onion. chopped

1/2 C. celery, chopped

1 clove garlic, minced

1 T. oil

4 C. beef broth

1 8-oz. can tomato sauce

1/4 t. oregano leaves

1 medium green pepper,
    chopped

1 C. zucchini, sliced

1 C. frozen corn

large can tomatoes

cheese, shredded (optional)

Mix meatball ingredients. Shape into about 30 meatballs.

Mix all soup ingredients and bring to a boil. Add meatballs. Cover and simmer 20 minutes. Serves 6. If desired, add shredded cheese before serving.

**—BEAVER BEND B & B,
FAIRBANKS**

OLD FASHIONED VENISON VEGETABLE SOUP

3 lbs. soup bones

2 qts. water

1 bay leaf

2 T. Season-All

1 t. celery salt

1/2 t. black pepper

1/4 t. thyme leaves

1/2 t. savory

1/4 t. MSG (optional)

1 T. beef-flavored base

1/4 C. chopped instant onions

2 C. tomatoes (one #303 can)

1 C. carrots, sliced

1/2 C. celery, chopped

2 C. potatoes, diced

2 C. corn

1 C. venison, cooked and diced
   (leftover venison roast is good
   to use)

Put soup bones in a large saucepan; add water and bay leaf. Bring to a boil and simmer 45 minutes, then add remaining ingredients and simmer covered for 3 hours. Remove bones. Serve piping hot.

**—BOWEY'S BED & BREAKFAST
KETCHIKAN**

THAI HOT AND SOUR SHRIMP SOUP

10 medium shrimp

1 qt. water

1 stalk lemon grass

1 C. button mushrooms (canned)

1 large onion, sliced

1/2 t. salt

1/2 t. MSG

2 T. fish sauce (Nampla)

2 T. lime juice

half a green or red chili pepper,

   chopped

8 coriander leaves (garnish)

cooked rice

Wash, peel and cut up shrimp. Bring the water to a boil and add lemon grass. Drop in shrimp and simmer for 3 minutes. Add all remaining ingredients and stir. Remove from heat. Serve in individual dishes. Garnish with coriander leaves. Serve hot with rice.

**—BEST OF ALL B & B,
VALDEZ**

CHAPTER 6

Furred, Feathered, Finned or On the Half Shell

MEAT

MINER'S BISCUITS AND GRAVY

1 lb. sausage

1 onion

chopped parsley

dash garlic powder

1/2 t. sage

salt and pepper to taste

dash Worcestershire sauce

1/4 C. flour

4 C. milk

Brown sausage. Add onion and parsley and saute until onion is transparent. Add spices and Worcestershire sauce. Add flour and cook a few more minutes. Add milk; bring almost to a boil and cook, stirring, until mixture thickens. Serve hot over your favorite biscuits.

—BACKWOODS B & B, HOMER

STUFFED PORK LOIN

pork loin

prunes

1 C. water

1/4 C. vinegar

1/2 C. sugar

nuts

apples

seasoned bread crumbs

Choose quantities of ingredients to suit taste and number of servings needed. Split pork loin lengthwise. Cook prunes in water, vinegar and sugar for 20 minutes, then force through sieve. Mix sieved mixture with nuts, apples and seasoned bread crumbs. Stuff loin, tie with twine and bake at 250 degrees for 2 hours.

—ALASKA RAINBOW LODGE, KVICHAK RIVER

PORK CHOP BAKE

6 slices bacon, coarsely chopped

1 lb. potatoes, peeled and sliced

   1/3-inch thick

1 lb. onions, sliced 1/3 inch-thick

1 lb. carrots, peeled and halved

   lengthwise and crosswise

6 (3/4-inch thick) loin pork

   chops, fat trimmed

2 C. beef broth

3 T. dry sherry

3 med. cloves garlic, minced

1 1/2 t. ginger, finely minced or

   grated

1/3 C. flour

1 t. salt

1/2 t. pepper

1/2 C. heavy cream

Scatter bacon over bottom of large deep skillet with domed cover or 13- x 9-inch oven-to-table casserole. Layer the potatoes, onions, carrots and pork chops in skillet.

In small bowl, combine 1 cup beef broth, sherry, garlic and ginger; pour over pork chops and cover with a tight lid or aluminum foil.

Bake at 350 degrees 1 hour or until carrots are easily pierced with a fork and meat is almost tender. Remove from oven and carefully remove cover. Increase temperature to 375 degrees. Place uncovered skillet in oven; bake 10 to 15 minutes longer or until pork chops are lightly browned.

Carefully tilt skillet over a bowl to drain off liquid (or use a turkey baster). Skim off the fat; measure and reserve 1 cup cooking liquid. In small pan over low heat combine flour, salt and pepper; gradually whisk in cream until smooth. Whisk in reserved liquid and bring to boiling for 1 minute, stirring constantly. Pour sauce over pork chops. Serves 6.

**—MEYERS CHUCK LODGE,
MEYERS CHUCK**

SEPTEMBER SWISS STEAK

Large 1-inch thick round steak
   cut into serving size pieces
salt and pepper
flour
1 medium onion, chopped
3 T. oil or bacon drippings
2 15-oz. cans of tomatoes
1 small can of mushrooms,
   drained

Salt and pepper meat, dredge in flour. In large iron skillet saute onion in oil or bacon drippings. Remove onion and set aside. Brown meat well on both sides. Set aside. Add 1 can of tomatoes to skillet and scrape bottom well to mix in drippings from meat. Stir in onion and mushrooms. Add meat and pour second can of tomatoes over top. Cover and simmer until tender (about 1 hour). Serve with potatoes or rice, using sauce as gravy.

—**TIMBERLINGS B & B,**
PALMER

STEAK DIANE

2 lbs. sirloin steak, sliced thin,
   trimmed and pounded
1/2 C. butter
handful of chives
parsley
salt and pepper to taste
1 scant t. Dijon mustard
Worcestershire sauce

Cook steaks in skillet on high heat for 1 to 2 minutes on each side. Meanwhile, in a small skillet or saucepan, melt butter; add remaining ingredients to make sauce. Spoon sauce over steaks and serve.

—**DENALI WEST LODGE,**
LAKE MINCHUMINA

CHICKEN-FRIED STEAK ALMONDINE

1 1/2 lbs. beef or caribou round steak, cut 1/2 inch thick

1 egg, beaten

1 T. milk

1 C. flour

3/4 C. almonds, finely chopped

1/2 t. salt

1/4 t. pepper

1 C. cooking oil

Cut steak into 6 pieces. Pound to 1/4-inch thick. Beat egg with milk. Combine flour, almonds, salt and pepper. Dip meat in egg mixture, then in flour mixture. In a deep skillet brown meat in hot oil, turning once. Cover, cook over low heat 45 to 60 minutes or until tender. Serves 6.

—ILIASKA LODGE, ILIAMNA LAKE

EASY QUICHE LORRAINE

12 slices bacon, crisply fried and crumbled

1 C. Swiss cheese, shredded

1/3 C. onion, chopped

2 C. milk

1 C. Bisquick

4 eggs

1/4 t. salt

1/8 t. pepper

Grease 10- x 1-1/2-inch quiche dish or pie pan. Sprinkle bacon, cheese and onion in pan. Beat remaining ingredients until smooth—15 seconds in blender or 1 minute on high with hand beater. Pour into pan. Bake at 400 degrees until knife inserted in center comes out clean, 35 to 40 minutes. Cool 5 minutes.

—EDE DEN B & B, WASILLA

POULTRY

CHICKEN WITH MUSHROOMS AND FIDDLEHEADS

2 C. fiddlehead ferns, cleaned (see note)

6 T. butter

3 T. flour

1 C. mushrooms, sliced

1 C. chicken stock, preferably homemade

2 1/2 C. cooked chicken, sliced thin

2 T. parsley

2 T. bread crumbs

Blanch the fiddleheads in slightly salted water for 1 to 2 minutes. Reduce heat and simmer until tender. Drain. Mix 3 tablespoons butter and flour in a saucepan and stir over medium heat. Add the broth and stir until sauce is smooth and thick. Saute the mushrooms in the remaining 3 tablespoons butter; add the mushrooms to the broth. Arrange fiddleheads in a buttered casserole dish. Lay chicken slices on top. Pour the sauce over the chicken. Sprinkle with bread crumbs and parsley. Bake at 350 degrees 30 minutes or until bubbly.

Note: Substitute asparagus or broccoli if you don't have fiddlehead ferns.

—RIVERSONG LODGE, YENTNA RIVER

CHICKEN FETTUCINE

1/4 C. butter

1 clove of garlic, minced

1 lb. chicken breasts, finely diced

1 bunch broccoli, cut in pieces

1/2 C. sour cream

2 C. whipping cream

salt and pepper to taste

3/4 C. Parmesan cheese, grated

5/8 lb. fresh fettucine (spinach
   or regular)

In large frying pan, melt butter and add garlic, chicken, and broccoli. Cook until tender. Mix in sour cream. Add whipping cream, salt and pepper. Cook until sauce is reduced by one-half, then add Parmesan cheese and mix well. Cook and drain fettucine, add to sauce, toss well, and serve.

**—WALLIN'S HILLTOP B & B,
ANCHOR POINT**

CHICKEN PAPRIKA

1 frying chicken, cut up and
   skinned

flour

salt and pepper

4 T. oil

1 medium onion, diced

1 sweet red pepper, diced

1 T. paprika

1/2 C. chicken broth

1/4 C. flour

1 C. sour cream

Mix flour, salt and pepper. Dredge chicken in flour. Brown in oil. Sprinkle with onion, pepper and paprika. Pour on broth. Cover and simmer 30 to 40 minutes. Remove chicken; keep warm. Stir 1/4 cup flour into pan drippings (add water if needed.) Cook, stirring constantly, until thick. Stir in sour cream. Heat through and pour over chicken. Serve with noodles or rice. Serves 4.

**—TUTKA BAY LODGE,
TUTKA BAY**

GAME HEN AND WILD RICE

1 game hen, thawed and split

3/4 C. teriyaki sauce

1/4 C. lemon juice

3/4 C. soy sauce

1 T. French dressing

1 small onion

1 carrot

2 celery stalks

1 small can water chestnuts

1 pkg. prepared wild rice mix

1 orange, sliced (garnish)

1 t. fresh parsley (garnish)

sesame seeds (garnish)

Combine liquids and marinate game hen halves for at least 1 hour. Bake hens in marinade at 325 degrees for 45 minutes, basting occasionally. Turn over, baste and continue cooking another 30 minutes.

Thinly slice carrot, celery and water chestnuts on the diagonal. Prepare rice according to package directions, adding vegetables. Place half of rice in each of two deep plates and position one hen half on top. Garnish with orange slices and fresh parsley, then sprinkle with sesame seeds. Serves 2.

—ALL THE COMFORTS OF HOME, ANCHORAGE

BAKED CHICKEN AND CORN

1 3 1/2-lb. chicken

salt and pepper

2 T. butter

2 16-oz. cans whole kernel corn

milk

1/2 C. dry bread crumbs

2 eggs, slightly beaten

1/2 t. salt

Cut up chicken and season with salt and pepper. Brown on all sides in butter in large skillet over medium heat.

Drain corn. Measure liquid and add milk to make 1 1/2 cups. Combine crumbs, corn, eggs and salt; slowly stir in milk mixture. Spread evenly in 2-quart greased casserole dish.

Arrange chicken on top. Pour drippings from skillet over all. Bake uncovered at 350 degrees until chicken is tender, about 1 hour. Serves 4.

—BETTY'S B & B,
FAIRBANKS

MAKE-AHEAD MACARONI

1 C. macaroni, uncooked

3/4 C. cooked chicken, turkey or
   ham, chopped

1 can cream of mushroom soup

2 C. milk

1 C. cheese, shredded

Combine all ingredients and pour into a greased 9- x 13-inch baking dish. Cover and refrigerate at least 8 hours. Uncover; bake at 350 degrees for 1 hour. Serves 3 or 4.

—WINDSOCK INN B & B,
JUNEAU

SEAFOOD

HALIBUT HASH

10 medium red potatoes,
  cooked, cooled and quartered

1 green pepper, chopped

1 red pepper, chopped

1 onion, chopped

1 lb. halibut

8 eggs

In large skillet, fry peppers and onion with potatoes in small amount of cooking oil. Add halibut and cook, breaking up fish into chunks as it cooks. While cooking hash, poach eggs in water. Top hash with poached eggs and serve.

—BLUEBERRY LODGE B & B,
JUNEAU

HALIBUT WITH LEMON CURRY SAUCE

1 C. mayonnaise

1 C. sour cream

1/4 C. dry sherry

1/4 t. curry powder

2 T. fresh lemon juice

1/2 C. onion, thinly sliced

2 lbs. halibut fillet pieces

1 small lemon, sliced thin

parsley sprigs (garnish)

Stir together mayonnaise, sour cream, sherry, curry powder, and lemon juice. Scatter onion in a large baking dish, arrange halibut on top and spread the mayonnaise mixture evenly over the halibut. Arrange the lemon slices on top and bake at 350 degrees for 30 to 35 minutes, or until fish just flakes. Garnish with parsley. Serves 6 to 8.

—TUTKA BAY LODGE,
HOMER

AL'S HALIBUT SUPREME

3 to 4 lbs. fresh halibut

2 T. butter

2 cloves garlic, finely chopped

2 T. flour

2 C. milk

1 t. salt

1/2 t. pepper

1/8 C. fresh parsley, finely
   chopped

1/2 t. fresh dill weed, chopped
   (optional)

1/4 C. fresh chives

1/4 C. Parmesan cheese

8 oz. crab meat

6 oz. mushrooms

2 T. butter

Cut fish into 6 serving pieces (about 1 inch thick) and set aside. In skillet, melt 2 tablespoons of butter and saute garlic, being careful not to scorch. Add flour to make a roux; gradually add milk and cook until medium thick. Add salt, pepper, parsley, dill weed, chives and Parmesan cheese. Keep warm. Saute crab meat and mushrooms in 2 tablespoons butter. Keep warm.

Bake halibut at 400 degrees for 10 minutes per inch of thickness. Do not overbake. Remove from oven. Smother fish with sauce, top with crab and mushrooms. Serves 6.

**—GLACIER BAY COUNTRY INN,
GUSTAVUS**

CLAY'S HALIBUT PECAN

4 pieces halibut fillet

1/2 C. mayonnaise

1 t. lemon pepper

1 t. dill

1/2 C. pecans, chopped

Blend mayonnaise, pepper and dill; spread over fillets. Press pecans on fillets and bake at 425 degrees 15 to 20 minutes.

**—CLAY'S QUALITY B & B,
HOMER**

HALIBUT FLORENTINE

1 box frozen spinach, cooked

1 t. basil

1 T. butter, melted

halibut fillets

2 egg whites

3 T. mayonnaise

1 T. Parmesan cheese

Drain spinach. Toss with basil and butter. Spread in 9-inch baking dish; cover with halibut. Beat egg whites until stiff. Fold in mayonnaise and Parmesan cheese. Spread mixture over fillets. Bake at 425 degrees for 10 to 15 minutes.

**—MARLOW'S KENAI RIVER
B & B, SOLDOTNA**

POACHED FRESH HALIBUT

halibut fillet (1 to 2 lbs.)

3 C. water

1 T. sugar

butter

lemon juice (optional)

garlic, minced (optional)

Skin fish and cut into 1-inch chunks. In medium pot, bring water and sugar to a boil. Put halibut into boiling water, about 8 to 10 pieces at a time, cover and cook about 2 minutes or until flaky and opaque (white in appearance). Dip in butter, melted with lemon juice and garlic, if desired.

**—LISIANSKI LODGE &
CHARTERS, PELICAN**

HALIBUT STUFFED WITH CRAB

4 pieces halibut fillet, about

   3- x 5- x 1-inch thick

1 lb. Dungeness crab meat

3 eggs

1/2 C. fine bread crumbs

1/2 t. white pepper

1/2 t. salt

1/2 t. Tabasco sauce

2 T. butter, melted

Cut a deep pocket into the side of each halibut piece. Mix the crab, eggs, bread crumbs and seasonings together. Put one-quarter of the mixture into the pocket of each fillet and place fish in a baking dish. Pour 1/2 tablespoon of melted butter over each fillet. Measure the thickness of the fish; broil or bake at 425 degrees for 10 minutes per inch of thickness.

—GLACIER BAY COUNTRY INN,
GUSTAVUS

ARCTIC CHAR IN LEEK SAUCE

arctic char (other white fish

   may be substituted)

1 egg beaten with 1 T. water

Panko (Japanese) bread crumbs

butter

3 leeks, cut into julienne strips

heavy cream

Clean and cut fish into serving-size pieces. Dip in egg wash, roll in bread crumbs. Saute in butter on medium-high heat until lightly browned on both sides. Remove fish. Saute julienned leeks in butter until translucent. Add heavy cream. Cook until thickened. Arrange char on warmed plate and pour sauce over top.

—ALASKA RAINBOW LODGE,
KING SALMON

ARCTIC LOON CRAB SOUFFLE

2 C. snow crab (thawed and
    drained if frozen)

10 eggs

2 C. large curd cottage cheese

3/4 C. Cheddar cheese, shredded

10 eggs

1 C. milk

2 T. dry sherry

Preheat oven to 350 degrees. Combine all ingredients and place in a greased 9- by 12-inch baking dish. Bake one hour. Delicious with croissants and strawberries.

**—ARCTIC LOON B & B,
ANCHORAGE**

BROILED CRAB SANDWICHES

4 sourdough English muffins

1 C. crab meat, flaked

1 C. Jack cheese, grated

1/2 C. mayonnaise

2 T. onion, chopped

1/4 C. celery, diced

1/8 t. garlic powder

1 T. parsley, snipped

Split muffins, butter and toast under broiler. Combine remaining ingredients and spread on muffin halves. Broil until bubbly. Serves 4.

**—TUTKA BAY LODGE,
HOMER**

BAKED BARBECUED SALMON

whole salmon

bread crumbs

onions

parsley

mushrooms

1 egg

bacon strips

butter, melted

lemon juice

wine

barbecue sauce

Combine bread crumbs, onions, parsley, mushrooms and egg. Stuff whole salmon (sockeye preferred) with mixture. Wrap salmon with bacon strips; place in baking dish and baste with butter, lemon juice and wine. Bake at 325 degrees for about 2 hours (total time will depend on thickness of fish). Baste every 20 to 30 minutes. Use your favorite barbecue sauce for final baste.

—BIG SKY CHARTER AND FISH
CAMP, STERLING

CATHY'S BAKED SALMON

6 to 8 lbs. salmon fillets, skin
    removed

1 egg, beaten

2 T. milk

2 C. Ritz crackers, crushed

Yoshida's Gourmet Sauce

Mix egg with milk, dip salmon fillets in egg mixture and then in crushed Ritz crackers. Place

in baking dish, cover and bake at 350 degrees for 15 to 20 minutes depending on thickness of salmon. Uncover, lightly drizzle just enough Yoshida's Gourmet Sauce over salmon to coat tops. Uncover and bake about 15 minutes longer.

—NORTHWOODS LODGE,
EAGLE RIVER

SALMON WITH SESAME-SCENTED HOLLANDAISE

1 king or silver salmon, cleaned
and filleted

salt and pepper

dry white wine

sesame seeds, toasted

Sesame-scented Hollandaise:

4 egg yolks

1 t. lemon juice

4 dashes Tabasco

1/4 t. salt

1/2 C. unsalted butter, melted

2 T. sesame oil

Place fillets skin side down in a buttered jelly roll pan. With tweezers or pliers, pull all pin bones and season with salt and pepper. Pour in just enough wine to cover bottom of baking pan and bake the fish at 400 degrees until thickest part registers 110 degrees with instant-read thermometer. (Depending on size of fish, this may only take 10 to 25 minutes to cook.) Remove fish from oven and transfer to serving platter. Lightly coat fillets with sesame-scented hollandaise and sprinkle with toasted sesame seeds.

Sesame-scented Hollandaise:
In top of double boiler, whisk together yolks, lemon juice, Tabasco and salt until thick and pale yellow—be careful of too much heat or eggs will scramble. When thick and fluffy remove from heat and scrape into food processor. With metal blade running, very slowly pour in the hot, melted butter and sesame oil. Season to taste after all the butter is mixed in. Makes 1 1/2 cups.

**—RIVERSONG LODGE,
YENTNA RIVER**

GRAVLAX-CURED SALMON FILLETS

2 lbs. fresh salmon fillets

1/4 C. salt

1/2 C. sugar

1 bunch dill, coarsely chopped

2 t. white peppercorns, crushed

Gravlax Sauce:

3 T. oil

1 T. red wine vinegar

1 T. sugar

1/3 t. salt

pinch of white pepper

2 to 3 T. prepared mustard

2 to 3 T. fresh dill, minced

Scale and debone salmon, cutting the fish into 2 pieces along the line of the backbone. Do not rinse, but wipe dry with paper towels. Mix salt and sugar and rub the fish with some of the mixture. Sprinkle part of the mixture and some of the dill in a deep enamel or earthenware baking dish. Place half of salmon, skin side down, in the dish and sprinkle generously with dill, crushed peppercorns, and salt/sugar mixture. Cover with remaining salmon, skin side up.

Sprinkle the salmon with the remaining salt/sugar mixture. Cover with a sheet of aluminum foil and a light weight such as a chopping board. The liquid should be poured off in about 4 to 5 hours. Keep the gravlax refrigerated for at least 48 hours, turning the fish around at least twice during this period. It can be stored for a week, and if properly chilled, should keep for 2 weeks.

To serve, cut into thin slices free from the skin. (Saute rolled up skin to use as garnish if desired.) Garnish with sliced cucumbers, dill and lemon wedges. Serve with gravlax sauce.

Gravlax Sauce: Blend all sauce ingredients except dill. Add the dill right before serving, or serve it in a separate bowl.

—ILIASKA LODGE,
ILIAMNA LAKE

SALMON WITH SAUCE BON FEMME

4 8-oz. salmon fillets (or other
    fish of choice)

1 pint white wine

1/2 C. onions, diced

3/4 C. fresh mushrooms, diced

1 pt. whipping cream

Poach fish fillets in boiling white wine for 3 minutes (fish should not be completely cooked), remove and set aside.

To make sauce Bon Femme, add diced onions and mushrooms to wine; reduce to 1 cup. Add cream and reduce again to 1 cup.

Poached fillets can be grilled over hot coals or broiled in oven till done. If grilling over coals, fillets should be coated with vegetable oil before placing on grill.

Add hot sauce to cover fish and serve. Serves 4.

—DENALI WILDERNESS LODGE, DENALI PARK

HONEY-LIME SALMON

1 C. lime juice

1/2 C. honey

2 t. Worcestershire sauce

2 cloves garlic, chopped fine

1/2 T. soy sauce

1/2 t. salt

2 fresh salmon fillets, skinned

lime slices (for garnish)

Mix first 6 ingredients and pour over fillets. Marinate the salmon for at least 4 hours. Remove fish from marinade and bake in a shallow pan for about 20 minutes at 375 degrees, basting often with marinade. Garnish with thinly sliced limes.

—ILIASKA LODGE, ILIAMNA LAKE

RIVERSONG SALMON BURGERS

*1 lb. boneless, skinless salmon,
steamed 5 to 7 minutes,
cooled and flaked (see note)*

*1/4 to 1/2 lb. smoked salmon,
flaked*

1/2 C. fresh bread crumbs

1 C. saltines, crushed

1 t. paprika

1/2 t. Tabasco

1 T. Worcestershire sauce

1 T. prepared mustard

2 T. lemon juice

1/2 t. salt

1/2 t. pepper

4 cloves garlic, crushed

1/2 C. scallions, finely chopped

1/4 C. parsley, finely chopped

1/3 C. celery, finely chopped

2 eggs, beaten

cornmeal

Mix all ingredients and form into patties, squeezing well. Dredge in cornmeal, and fry over medium high heat on both sides until brown and crispy. Serve with your favorite burger condiments or tartar sauce. Serves 10.

Note: As an alternative, leftover barbecued salmon is excellent in this recipe.

**—RIVERSONG LODGE,
YENTNA RIVER**

SALMON WITH DILL SAUCE

1 t. salt

1 medium onion, sliced

1 t. or 1 cube chicken bouillon

1 1/2 C. water

1 T. lemon juice

4 salmon steaks or fillets

Dill Sauce:

2 T. margarine or butter

1 T. onion, finely chopped

2 T. flour

1 t. salt

1 t. dill weed

1/8 t. pepper

1 1/2 C. milk

In a skillet large enough to hold fish in a single layer, combine first five ingredients. Heat to boiling. Add salmon and simmer, tightly covered, for 10 minutes or until fish flakes easily. Place fish on platter; pour Dill Sauce over fish and serve. Serves 4.

Dill Sauce: In a small saucepan, cook onion in margarine until tender; stir in flour, salt, dill weed and pepper. Add milk, mixing well. Heat until mixture boils and thickens, stirring constantly.

—KACHEMAK BAY WILDERNESS LODGE, CHINA POOT BAY

SALMON PUFF

4 eggs, slightly beaten

1/2 C. milk

1 can cream of mushroom soup

1 15 1/2-oz. can red salmon

2 C. soft bread crumbs

1 T. parsley

2 T. butter

Combine eggs, milk and soup. Blend in the remaining ingredients and place in a buttered casserole. Bake at 325 degrees for 40 to 50 minutes.

—BOWEY'S B & B KETCHIKAN

SHAN'S BARBECUED SALMON

6 to 8 lbs. salmon fillets

fresh ground pepper

4 T. honey or melted white wine jelly

Sauce:

1/4 lb. butter, melted

1/3 C. olive oil

4 garlic cloves, crushed

1 1/2 t. Worcestershire sauce

1 t. onion salt

2 dashes Tabasco sauce

1/4 C. dry white wine

juice of 1/2 lemon

1 T. stone ground mustard

Combine all sauce ingredients; set aside. Place salmon fillets skin side down on preheated barbecue grill. Pierce fish with fork in several places. Sprinkle liberally with fresh ground pepper and generously brush with sauce. Close barbecue lid. Brush sauce on fish every 5 minutes during cooking. Fish is done when it flakes easily, and has turned from semi-transparent dark pink to non-transparent light pink, about 20 minutes. Do not overcook. During last 5 minutes, brush honey or jelly on fish to glaze.

—NORTHWOODS LODGE, EAGLE RIVER

SALMON WITH VEGETABLE STUFFING

8 to 10 lb. salmon, cleaned

salad oil

Vegetable Stuffing:

2 medium onions, finely chopped

1/4 C. butter

2 C. dry bread cubes

1 C. carrots, coarsely shredded

1 C. mushrooms, washed and
* cut up*

1/2 C. parsley, chopped

1 1/2 T. lemon juice

1 egg

1 clove garlic, minced

2 t. salt

1/4 t. marjoram leaves

1/4 t. pepper

Baste:

1/2 C. butter, melted

1/4 C. lemon juice

Mix all stuffing ingredients together. Season fish with salt and pepper and stuff with vegetable stuffing. Brush fish with salad oil; place in shallow pan. Bake, uncovered, at 325 degrees for 1 to 1 1/2 hours or until fish flakes easily with fork. Baste fish occasionally with butter and lemon juice mixture. Makes 10 to 12 servings.

**—ILIASKA LODGE,
ILIAMNA LAKE**

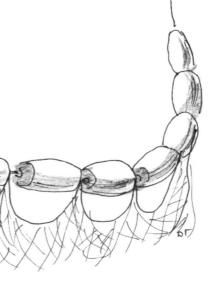

WILD RICE PAELLA WITH ALASKA SHRIMP

2 lbs. Alaska shrimp, cleaned
   and deveined

4 T. unsalted butter

1 large onion, chopped

2 cloves garlic, minced

a few threads of saffron

2 bay leaves

red pepper flakes

2 C. wild rice (soak if necessary)

6 C. combination chicken,
   shrimp and/or lobster stock

3 tomatoes, peeled and chopped

1 C. tiny sweet peas

1/2 C. chopped fresh herbs
   (basil, chives and parsley)

Saute shrimp in the butter until pink, remove from pan. Add onions and saute until translucent; add garlic, saffron, bay leaves and red pepper flakes to taste. Stir in wild rice and stock and bring to a boil. Cover and cook until rice is tender. Add shrimp with tomatoes and peas and stir gently. Correct seasonings and finish with fresh herbs.

—ALASKA RAINBOW LODGE,
KING SALMON

MARTHA'S PRAWNS LOUISIANNE

7 lbs. prawns, shells on

4 T. Tony's or Old Bay seasoning

2 C. butter, melted

1 C. lemon juice

1 C. white wine

Wash prawns; slice lengthwise in half, place in baking pans and sprinkle with seasoning. Mix butter, lemon juice and white wine; pour over all. Bake at 350 degrees until pink, 15 to 20 minutes. Serves 10 to 15.

—ILIASKA LODGE,
ILIAMNA LAKE

SHRIMP AND CHEESE DUMPLINGS

1 pkg. prepared pie crust mix

1/2 C. onion, chopped

3 T. butter or margarine

1/4 C. green pepper, finely
   chopped

1 C. celery, chopped

1/2 lb. shredded cheese

3/4 C. (1 5-oz. can) shrimp,
   cooked, shelled, deveined and
   cut into small pieces

Roll pastry 1/8-inch thick. Cut into 8 5-inch squares. Cook onion in butter until light golden brown. Add green pepper and celery. Cover tightly and simmer until celery is tender—about 10 minutes—stirring occasionally.

Remove cover. Add cheese and keep over very low heat until cheese is melted, stirring constantly. Remove from heat; add shrimp and mix well.

Place 1/4 cup cheese mixture in center of pastry square, moisten edge with cold water. Fold so that corners of square meet in center over mixture and press edges firmly together to prevent leakage of filling. Prick top in several places.

Bake at 400 degrees until light golden brown, about 20 to 25 minutes. Serve hot. I serve these with cheesed grits for breakfast.

—BETTY'S B & B,
FAIRBANKS

SEAFOOD FETTUCINE

1 lb. scallops

1 lb. shrimp, peeled

1 lb. squid, sliced

1/4 lb. Petersburg shrimp

1 1/2 lbs. halibut, cut into
    1-inch cubes

1 lb. salmon, cut into 1-inch
    cubes

1 C. onions, chopped

1 1/2 C. celery, chopped

1/2 C. olive oil

1/2 C. butter

6 cloves garlic, minced

1 t. white pepper

1/4 t. nutmeg

1/2 t. salt

2 C. cream

2 C. milk

2 C. Parmesan cheese

2 lbs. fettucine (dry weight)

fresh parsley

fresh chives

1/2 lb. crab meat (optional)

sliced lemons (garnish)

Prepare the seafood and set aside. In a 6-quart (or larger) stockpot, saute the onions and celery in the olive oil and butter for about 3 minutes. Add the garlic, white pepper, nutmeg and salt; saute until the onions and celery are tender. Stir in the scallops, peeled shrimp and squid; saute for 2 minutes. Stir in the Petersburg shrimp, halibut and salmon; saute for 2 more minutes. Add the cream and milk and bring just to a simmer. Add the Parmesan cheese, stirring gently so as not to break up the fish.

Cook fettucine just until tender; drain and rinse. On each plate, place fettucine, cover with sauce, top with fresh parsley, chives and crab (if using). Garnish with sliced lemon. Serves 12.

—GLACIER BAY COUNTRY INN,
GUSTAVUS

HERB WAFFLES WITH SEAFOOD SAUCE

Waffles:

2 C. flour

1 T. baking powder

1/2 t. salt

2 C. milk

2 eggs, separated

1 T. fresh parsley

1 T. onion, finely chopped

1 t. fresh sage

1 t. fresh thyme

6 T. butter, melted

Seafood Sauce:

1/4 C. butter

1/4 C. onion, chopped

1/4 C. celery, chopped

3 T. flour

1 to 2 C. broth

1 C. milk

1 lb. fresh seafood (shrimp, crab,
   or salmon), cooked

1 T. lemon juice

salt and cracked pepper

fresh parsley (garnish)

Waffles: Combine dry ingredients, beat milk and egg yolks with herbs and add to dry ingredients along with the butter. Fold in beaten egg whites just before cooking on a hot, greased waffle iron.

Seafood Sauce: Saute vegetables in butter. Add flour, then broth and milk, and cook, stirring often, until thickened. Add seafood, lemon juice and salt and pepper to taste; reheat while stirring. Spoon sauce over hot waffles, garnish with parsley and serve.

**—MAGIC CANYON RANCH
B & B, HOMER**

CRAB QUICHE

1 C. fine soda cracker crumbs

1/4 C. margarine, melted

2 eggs, beaten

3/4 C. IMO (sour cream
   substitute)

1/4 t. salt

1/4 t. pepper

1 C. onion, chopped

2 C. Swiss cheese, grated

1/2 C. Cheddar cheese, grated

1 C. crab meat

6 slices bacon, fried crisp and
   crumbled

Combine crumbs and margarine and press into bottom and sides of an 8-inch pie pan. Mix remaining ingredients, pour into pie shell and bake at 375 degrees for 25 to 30 minutes or until knife inserted in center comes out clean.

—**CREEK'S EDGE B & B,
SITKA**

HALIBUT PIE

1 C. halibut, cooked

1 C. Cheddar cheese, shredded

3 oz. cream cheese, cubed

1/4 C. green onions, sliced

2 C. milk

1 C. Bisquick baking mix

4 eggs

3/4 t. salt

Grease a 10-inch pie pan. Layer halibut, cheeses and onions in pan. In a blender combine remaining ingredients and blend on high for 15 seconds (or 1 minute with hand beater). Pour into plate. Bake at 400 degrees 35 to 40 minutes or until knife inserted near center comes out clean. Cool 5 minutes. Makes 6 to 8 servings.

Variation: Use salmon, crab or shrimp in place of halibut.

**—ANCHOR RIVER B & B,
ANCHOR POINT**

CRUSTLESS SALMON QUICHE

4 eggs

2 C. evaporated milk

2 t. dill weed

2 T. onion, chopped

salt and pepper to taste

1 1-lb. can salmon, flaked

1/2 C. Swiss cheese, grated

Beat eggs with milk. Add all ingredients except cheese. Sprinkle cheese in bottom of pie pan. Pour egg mixture on top of cheese. Bake at 425 degrees 15 minutes, then 325 degrees for 40 minutes.

**—LION'S DEN WILDERNESS
LODGE, KODIAK**

7 GABLES SALMON QUICHE

2 ready-made pie crusts,
  unbaked

1 C. salmon, cooked and flaked

4 green onions, chopped

8 eggs

4 C. whipping cream

1/2 t. sugar

1/4 t. cayenne pepper

Scatter salmon and onions evenly in the two crusts. Beat eggs well; add whipping cream, sugar and cayenne. Pour half of mixture over salmon in each crust. Bake at 425 degrees for 15 minutes. Reduce heat to 300 degrees and bake another 45 minutes. Cool 10 minutes before cutting. Serves 12.

**—ALASKA'S 7 GABLES B & B,
FAIRBANKS**

WHISPERING POND SALMON QUICHE

1/2 C. mayonnaise

1 1/2 C. salmon, cooked or
  canned

2 T. flour

2 eggs, beaten

1 1/2 C. cheese, grated (any
  kind)

1/2 C. milk

1/3 C. green onions

several sliced mushrooms

1 9-inch ready-made pie crust,
  unbaked

Combine all ingredients and pour into pie shell. Bake at 350 degrees for 40 to 45 minutes, or until knife inserted near center comes out clean.

**—WHISPERING POND B & B,
SOLDOTNA**

MAGIC CANYON QUICHE

Pie Crusts:

1 C. wheat germ

3 C. whole wheat pastry flour

1 T. salt

1 C. shortening

1 T. honey

1 T. vinegar

1 egg

warm water

Filling:

24 oz. Swiss cheese, grated

1 lb. cooked salmon (fresh or
  canned)

1 lb. fresh broccoli flowerettes

salt

fresh chives

fresh cracked pepper

6 C. milk

9 eggs

Pie crusts: Mix wheat germ, flour and salt; cut in shortening. Mix honey, vinegar and egg; add enough warm water to make 1 cup liquid. Mix into dry ingredients. Form into 3 balls, wrap in plastic and chill overnight. Roll out dough and line 3 9-inch quiche pans.

Filling: Cover bottom of crusts with a bit of shredded cheese. Add salmon, broccoli, salt, chives, and remaining cheese. Blend 2 cups milk and 3 eggs for each quiche. Top with cracked pepper. Bake at 375 degrees for 15 minutes, then at 350 degrees for 45 minutes. Cool before serving. Makes 3 9-inch quiches.

—MAGIC CANYON RANCH
B & B, HOMER

EGGS AND CHEESE

BROCCOLI QUICHE

Crust:

1 C. margarine

4 oz. cream cheese

2 C. flour

Dijon mustard

Filling:

1 bunch (about 1 lb.) broccoli

1 C. cream

1 C. milk

4 eggs

1 C. Monterey Jack cheese,

   grated

salt and pepper

Crust: Mix margarine and cream cheese. Cut in the flour. Fit into a deep 10-inch quiche pan and bake at 425 degrees for 15 minutes. Brush with Dijon mustard and bake another 2 to 3 minutes.

Filling: Cut broccoli into pieces and blanch in boiling water for 5 minutes. Drain, cool and chop coarsely. Mix cream, milk and eggs. Add broccoli, cheese and salt and pepper to taste. Pour into pastry shell. Bake at 375 degrees for 30 minutes.

**—VILLAGE STRIP B & B,
TALKEETNA**

CRUSTLESS MUSHROOM CHEESE QUICHE

1/2 C. butter

1 lb. mushrooms, sliced

10 eggs

1 pt. cottage cheese

1 lb. Monterey Jack cheese,
   shredded

1/2 C. flour

1 t. baking powder

1/2 t. salt

Melt butter in large pan. Remove from heat and cool slightly. Add mushrooms and toss gently to coat (do not saute) set aside. Beat eggs in large bowl. Add cottage cheese, Jack cheese, flour, baking powder and salt. Mix thoroughly. Stir in mushrooms. Pour into a greased 9- x 13-inch baking pan. Bake at 350 degrees 45 to 50 minutes.

—HATCHER PASS B & B,
PALMER

QUICHE WITH OLIVE AND MUSHROOM CRUST

Crust:

1/2 lb. mushrooms, chopped

3/4 C. black olives, chopped

3 T. butter

1/4 C. fine cracker or bread
   crumbs

Filling:

1/2 C. black olives, sliced

1/2 C. green onions, chopped

6 oz. Swiss cheese, grated

1 C. cottage cheese

3 eggs

1/2 t. thyme

Crust: Saute mushrooms and chopped olives in butter about half a minute, then stir in crumbs. Press against bottom and sides 9-inch quiche pan or pie pan to make crust.

Filling: Mix olives, onions and Swiss cheese; sprinkle into crust. Mix cottage cheese, eggs and thyme in blender. Pour over ingredients in crust. Bake in lower half of oven at 375 degrees for about 25 minutes or until knife inserted in center comes out dry. Let stand 10 minutes before serving.
Serves 6.

**—TIMBERLINGS B & B,
PALMER**

—CHAPTER 7—

From the Garden

POTATOES, RICE AND PASTA

ACCORDION POTATOES

10 medium-sized potatoes

1/2 C. butter, melted

2 t. salt

1/8 t. pepper

3 t. paprika

Peel potatoes. Make thin cuts one half inch apart, about 3/4 of the way through from top to bottom, leaving bottom of potato whole. Dry well and roll potatoes in melted butter. Place in roasting pan and bake at 375 degrees for 2 1/2 hours. Sprinkle with salt and pepper; baste often with melted butter. After about 2 hours of roasting, sprinkle potatoes with paprika. Continue roasting until done. Serves 10.

**—ILIASKA LODGE,
ILIAMNA LAKE**

BAKED POTATO CASSEROLE

6 medium or 4 large potatoes

1 t. salt

1 C. sour cream

6 to 8 fresh green onions,
   chopped with some greens
   (can substitute parsley)

1 C. (4 oz.) Cheddar cheese,
   shredded

1/2 t. onion salt

1/4 C. butter, melted

Peel, quarter and boil potatoes until barely tender. Drain, cool, and grate on large side of grater. Place in large bowl. Gently mix in all other ingredients, except butter. Place mixture into a greased shallow pan. Top with melted butter. Bake at 350 degrees for 20 to 30 minutes, or until golden. Serves 6 to 8.

**—TUTKA BAY LODGE,
HOMER**

HASH BROWN CASSEROLE

2-lb. pkg. frozen hash browns

1 can cream of mushroom soup

1 can cream of chicken or cream
of celery soup

1 pt. sour cream (with chives if
desired)

1/2 C. milk

4 oz. Cheddar cheese, grated

Mix all ingredients except cheese. Put in 9- x 13-inch baking dish and bake at 350 degrees for 45 minutes. Remove from oven; sprinkle cheese over top of casserole. Return to oven and bake an additional 15 minutes. Serves 10 to 12. Good served with eggs, ham, bacon or sausage.

**—ARCTIC TERN B & B,
SOLDOTNA**

COUNTRY INN SAUTEED POTATOES

4 C. potatoes, diced (preferably
new potatoes)

1/2 C. butter

1/4 C. chives, chopped

1/4 C. parsley, chopped

1 t. salt

1/2 t. white pepper

1/2 t. fresh dill weed (optional)

If you are using freshly dug potatoes, there is no need to peel them, just scrub well. Heat 1 inch of water to boiling in large saucepan; add potatoes. Cover and cook just until tender, about 20 minutes. Drain and plunge in cold water to stop cooking. Melt butter in skillet; add potatoes and seasonings. Stir gently to coat potatoes; heat through. Serve immediately. Serves 8.

**—GLACIER BAY COUNTRY INN,
GUSTAVUS**

HEAVENLY SPUDS

8 potatoes, peeled and sliced

1 1/2 C. sour cream

1 can cream of chicken soup

1 small onion, minced

2 T. butter, melted

1 t. salt

1/2 t. pepper

1/2 C. Cheddar cheese, grated

1 C. barbecue potato chips,
  crushed

Place potatoes in large casserole dish. Mix next 6 ingredients and pour over sliced potatoes. Bake at 350 degrees for 50 minutes or until tender. Sprinkle grated cheese and crushed potato chips over potatoes. Place back into oven until cheese melts. Serves 10 to 12.

**—CLAY'S QUALITY B & B,
HOMER**

PARMESAN CHEESE POTATOES

1/2 C. margarine

1 C. Parmesan cheese, grated

4 medium potatoes

sour cream

Melt margarine in a 13- x 9-inch pan. Sprinkle about 1/2 cup of the Parmesan cheese in margarine. Peel and cut potatoes into quarters. Roll in butter and cheese mixture. Sprinkle remaining Parmesan cheese over the top of potatoes and bake until done and crunchy outside, approximately 40 minutes. Serve with sour cream.

**—MEYERS CHUCK LODGE,
MEYERS CHUCK**

POTATO CAKES

1 pkg. hash browns with onions

2 eggs, well beaten

1/4 C. milk

2 T. flour

1 t. salt

dash pepper

Cover potatoes with hot water, let stand 5 minutes. Drain on paper towels. Mix remaining ingredients; stir in potatoes. Drop by tablespoonfuls on hot, well greased griddle. Cook 3 minutes on each side until brown.

**—EDE DEN B & B,
WASILLA**

LEMON POTATO WEDGES

1/2 t. dill weed

1 t. lemon peel, grated

3 t. lemon juice

1/4 C. butter, melted

4 potatoes, cooked and cooled

1/4 C. Parmesan cheese, grated

In a small bowl, combine dill, lemon peel, lemon juice and melted butter. Cut each potato lengthwise into 8 wedges. Place on baking sheet and brush with dill/lemon mixture. Sprinkle Parmesan cheese over wedges. Bake at 425 degrees for 20 minutes or until tender. Serve with sour cream. Serves 4.

**—CLAY'S QUALITY B & B,
HOMER**

HERBED LENTILS AND RICE

4 oz. Swiss cheese

2 2/3 C. chicken broth

3/4 C. dry lentils

3/4 C. onion, chopped

1/2 C. brown rice (uncooked)

1/4 C. dry white wine

1/2 t. dried basil, crushed

1/4 t. salt

1/4 t. dried oregano, crushed

1/8 t. pepper

1/8 t. garlic powder

1/4 t. thyme

Shred half of the Swiss cheese. Mix all ingredients and the shredded cheese, stirring well. Turn into a 1 1/2-quart casserole. Bake covered in a 350-degree oven for 1 1/2 to 2 hours, stirring twice during baking. Cut remaining cheese into 8 strips. Uncover casserole, top with cheese strips, and bake uncovered 2 to 3 minutes longer, until cheese is melted. Makes 4 servings.

—FAVORITE BAY INN,
ANGOON

RICE PILAF

1 C. long grain rice

1/4 C. onion, chopped

2 T. butter

1/2 C. mushrooms, sliced

1 t. chicken base

1/2 t. thyme

1/2 t. salt

2 C. cold water

Saute rice and onion in butter until golden. Add mushrooms. Add chicken base, thyme and salt to water; pour into rice. Cover with a tight-fitting lid. Bring to boiling; reduce heat. Cook 15 minutes; don't lift cover. Remove from heat; let stand covered for 10 minutes. Serves 6.

—ILIASKA LODGE,
ILIAMNA LAKE

LINGUINI CARBONARA

1 lb. linguine

6 eggs

1 C. grated Parmesan cheese

1 lb. bacon

10 oz. fresh mushrooms, sliced

1 C. heavy cream

Cook linguine, rinse and drain. Set aside. In separate bowl, beat eggs; add cheese. Cook bacon slowly; remove from pan and fry mushrooms in reserved drippings. Remove and drain. Stir egg mixture, bacon and mushrooms into cooked linguine. Fold in heavy cream. Pour into casserole dish and bake slowly at 160 to 200 degrees until hot (a higher temperature will cause the eggs to cook too quickly).

**—THE SUMMER INN B & B,
HAINES**

SALADS

AMBROSIA

2 cans Mandarin oranges with
  juice

1 C. green grapes

1 C. red grapes

4 bananas, sliced

1 C. shredded coconut

1/2 C. sugar

nutmeg

Combine first 5 ingredients in bowl; sprinkle sugar over top. Garnish with nutmeg and chill.

—ALL THE COMFORTS OF HOME, ANCHORAGE

OVERNIGHT COLESLAW

1 medium head cabbage

1 onion, grated

1 carrot, grated

1 green pepper, chopped
  (optional)

Dressing:

1 1/2 C. sugar

3/4 C. vinegar

3/4 C. vegetable oil

1 t. celery seed

salt and pepper to taste

Prepare vegetables; set aside. Combine dressing ingredients in saucepan; bring to boil. Do not cool. In large glass bowl or gallon jar, put layer of cabbage, layer of onion, layer of carrot, layer of green pepper. Pour hot dressing over vegetables. Repeat until all vegetables and dressing are used. Cover and refrigerate overnight before serving. Will keep for several days. Serves 12 to 16.

—GLACIER BAY COUNTRY INN, GUSTAVUS

MARINATED BROCCOLI SALAD

1 pkg. Good Seasons Italian
   salad dressing mix

1 T. Worcestershire sauce

1 T. soy sauce

1 lbs. fresh broccoli, stems
   peeled, cut in bite-size pieces

1/4 lb. fresh mushrooms, sliced

1 green onion, sliced

1 clove garlic, crushed

1/4 lb. Cheddar cheese, cut in
   small cubes

1 avocado, sliced

1 fresh tomato, cubed

Follow package directions for making Italian dressing, adding Worcestershire and soy sauces. Combine broccoli, mushrooms, onions, garlic and cheese in serving bowl. Pour half the dressing over the vegetables, refrigerate several hours. Just before serving, add avocado, tomato and remaining dressing. Makes 14 cups.

—**NORTHWOODS LODGE,
EAGLE RIVER**

BROCCOLI SALAD

2 bunches broccoli

3/4 C. red onion, chopped

3/4 C. honey roasted peanuts

3/4 C. raisins

Dressing:

1 C. mayonnaise

1/2 C. sugar

2 T. red wine vinegar

Cut broccoli into bite-size pieces. Combine broccoli, onion, peanuts and raisins. Mix dressing ingredients together and blend well. Pour dressing over broccoli, toss and serve.

—**MEYERS CHUCK LODGE,
MEYERS CHUCK**

DOROTHY'S ORIENTAL SALAD

2 T. butter

2 pkgs. Top Ramen

1/2 C. almonds, sliced

1/2 C. sesame seeds, toasted

1 head Nappa cabbage

6 green onions

Dressing:

1/2 C. peanut oil

1/4 C. wine vinegar

1 t. sesame oil

1/4 C. sugar

salt and pepper to taste

In melted butter, saute broken up Top Ramen noodles, almonds and sesame seeds until brown. Add Top Ramen seasoning. Slice cabbage and onions. Add noodle/nut mixture. Combine dressing ingredients, Pour over salad and toss.

—BARANOF ISLAND
WILDERNESS LODGE,
BARANOF ISLAND

RICE SALAD WITH CURRY AND ARTICHOKE HEARTS

1 pkg. chicken-flavored Rice-a-
Roni mix

1 whole small green pepper,
chopped

1/2 C. onion, chopped

2 6-oz. jars marinated artichoke
hearts, drained (reserve juice)
and chopped

1/2 C. mayonnaise

3/4 t. curry powder

Prepare Rice-a-Roni according to directions on package, omitting butter. To cooked rice, add green pepper, onion and artichoke hearts. Mix in mayonnaise, thinned with a little juice from the artichoke hearts, and curry powder.

—LISIANSKI LODGE,
PELICAN

ENCORE AVOCADO SALAD

Dressing:

juice of 1 lime

5 T. salad oil

salt and freshly ground pepper

1/2 t. to 2 t. chili pepper

Salad:

1 head butter lettuce

1 head red leaf lettuce

1 peeled avocado, sliced

1 jicama, about the same size as
  avocado, cut into same size
  slices (see note)

1/2 cantaloupe, peeled and cut
  into bite-sized chunks

Mix dressing ingredients together and set aside. In glass salad bowl, tear lettuce into small pieces; add avocado, jicama and cantaloupe.

Whisk dressing again and pour evenly over salad. Toss lightly before serving to combine well.

Note: If you cannot get jicama, substitute one small can of sliced water chestnuts.

**—TIMBERLINGS B & B,
PALMER**

ALICE'S ASPIC

1 can stewed tomatoes

1 small pkg. raspberry Jello

1 C. boiling water

1 C. chopped vegetables
  (carrots, onions, celery or
  green peppers separately or
  in combination)

Combine Jello and boiling water. Puree tomatoes in blender, add to dissolved Jello mixture. Add vegetables. Chill until firm, then serve.

**—ALL THE COMFORTS OF
HOME, ANCHORAGE**

GRILLED PTARMIGAN SALAD

2 ptarmigan (or Cornish game
   hen) breasts, cleaned and bled
salt and pepper

Salad:

1 head Boston bibb lettuce

1 head red leaf lettuce

Dressing:

1 pomegranate, juiced and seeds
   for garnish

2 T. red raspberry vinegar

2 cloves garlic, minced

salt and pepper

1 egg yolk (optional)

6 T. light olive oil

Garnish:

1 sweet Maui onion, cut into
   rings and placed in ice water

flour for dusting

3 C. oil for frying

1 zucchini squash, cut into
   julienne strips

1 cluster oyster mushrooms,
   sliced

1 T. sweet butter

red and black currants

After cleaning the ptarmigan breast grill to medium rare and season with salt and pepper; set aside and keep warm.

Clean the lettuce and rinse well, break into bite-size pieces reserving a few larger leaves.

Dressing: Whisk together pomegranate juice, vinegar, garlic and salt and pepper; add the olive oil in a slow and steady stream. (You may add an egg yolk before the olive oil to stabilize the dressing.)

Garnish: Dry onion rings well and dredge in flour. Heat oil to 350 degrees and fry rings until golden and crisp; drain.

Assembly: Slice meat on an angle and arrange fanned out on lettuce leaves on plates. Toss lettuce in the dressing mixture and arrange around meat. Decorate with mushrooms and zucchini, sauteed in butter, red and black currants and top with the onion rings. Serves 2.

**—ALASKA RAINBOW LODGE,
KING SALMON**

FRESH VEGETABLE SALAD

Salad:

1 head cauliflower, broken into
    flowerettes

1 bunch broccoli, chopped

carrots, sliced

1/2 C. raisins

radishes, chopped

green pepper, chopped

onion, chopped

1/2 lb. bacon, fried and
    crumbled

Dressing:

1/2 C. mayonnaise

1/2 t. each salt and pepper

1/3 C. oil

1/4 C. sugar

Toss together all the salad ingredients and refrigerate. Mix dressing ingredients together. Just before serving, toss salad with dressing.

**—LION'S DEN WILDERNESS
LODGE, KODIAK**

HOT GERMAN POTATO SALAD

6 medium potatoes, boiled,
    peeled and thinly sliced

3 slices bacon

3/4 C. chopped onion

2 T. flour

2 T. sugar

1 1/2 t. salt

1/2 t. celery seeds

dash of pepper

3/4 C. water

1/3 C. vinegar

Fry bacon; drain (reserve fat), crumble and set aside. Saute onion in bacon fat until golden brown. Blend in flour, sugar, salt, celery seeds and pepper. Cook over low heat, stirring until smooth. Remove from heat. Stir in water and vinegar. Heat to boiling, stirring constantly. Boil 1 minute. Gently stir in potato slices and bacon. Serves 6 to 8.

**—TUTKA BAY LODGE,
HOMER**

THREE BEAN SALAD

1 can wax beans

1 can green beans

1 can kidney beans

1 can garbanzo beans (optional)

1 onion, sliced

1 green pepper, sliced

salt and pepper to taste

Dressing:

3/4 C. sugar

2/3 C. vinegar

1/3 C. oil

Drain beans and place in bowl. Add onion, green pepper and salt and pepper.

Mix dressing ingredients together and pour over beans. Cover and refrigerate overnight for full flavor.

**—CLAY'S QUALITY B & B,
HOMER**

LAYERED GREEN SALAD

1/2 head lettuce, shredded

1/2 C. green onion, thinly sliced

1 C. celery, thinly sliced

1 8-oz. can water chestnuts,

thinly sliced

10 oz. frozen peas (defrosted)

Dressing:

1 to 2 C. mayonnaise

2 T. sugar

1 t. seasoning salt

1/4 t. garlic salt

1/2 C. Parmesan cheese

Toppings:

4 to 5 hard boiled eggs,

chopped

1/2 lb. bacon, fried crisp and

crumbled

3 or 4 tomatoes, chopped

Layer first 5 ingredients in glass bowl, in order given, ending with peas. Mix dressing ingredients together and spread over top. Sprinkle toppings over salad and refrigerate for 12 to 24 hours. Serves 8 to 12.

Variation: Substitute blue cheese for Parmesan cheese.

—MEYERS CHUCK LODGE, MEYERS CHUCK

MARINATED SHRIMP AND VEGETABLES

1 pound medium shrimp, raw

1 C. fresh cauliflowerettes

1/4 lb. small fresh mushrooms

1 C. zucchini, sliced

1 large red or green pepper

3/4 C. Realemon lemon juice

1 T. green onion, chopped

2 t. sugar

1 t. salt

1/4 to 1/2 t. dill weed

5 drops hot pepper sauce

3/4 C. vegetable oil

Peel and devein shrimp. Cook in boiling water until shrimp turns pink. Drain and cool. Place shrimp and vegetables in shallow dish. In a small bowl or jar combine the remaining ingredients, except oil. Mix well. Add oil and mix well. Pour over shrimp and vegetables. Cover and refrigerate for 6 hours. Makes about 5 cups.

**—QUIET PLACE LODGE B & B,
HALIBUT COVE**

MOLDED SHRIMP SALAD

1 pkg. (6 oz.) lemon Jello

1 C. hot water

1/2 C. whipping cream

1/2 C. mayonnaise

8 oz. cream cheese

1/2 C. stuffed olives, sliced

3 hard cooked eggs, chopped

1/2 C. celery

2 T. onion, chopped

1 C. shrimp, cooked

Mix the Jello and hot water, stirring to dissolve completely. Refrigerate. Blend cream, mayonnaise and cream cheese. When Jello starts to set, stir in the cream cheese mixture. Mix remaining ingredients together and add to Jello. Put into mold and let set up in refrigerator until firm.

**—WALLIN'S HILLTOP B & B,
ANCHOR POINT**

CRANBERRY ORANGE SALAD

1 pkg. cranberries (fresh or
   frozen)

1 orange, peeled

1/2 C. walnuts, chopped

1/2 to 1 C. sugar

Wash and sort cranberries, discarding bad ones. Run cranberries through coarse blade of grinder or process in food processor or blender. Cut orange into small pieces. Combine cranberries, oranges, walnuts and sugar (to taste) in bowl. Refrigerate several hours to meld flavors. Very good with poultry.

—GLACIER BAY COUNTRY INN, GUSTAVUS

ORIENTAL CABBAGE SALAD

2 T. sesame seeds, toasted

1/2 C. slivered almonds, toasted

1/2 head cabbage, chopped fine

3 to 4 green onions, sliced
   (optional)

1 pkg. Top Ramen noodles,
   crushed

Dressing:

2 T. sugar

1/2 C. oil

1/4 C. vinegar

flavoring packet from soup
   package (chicken is good)

Combine first 5 ingredients. Mix dressing ingredients and pour over salad. Let stand overnight.

—DENALI WEST LODGE, LAKE MINCHUMINA

PINEAPPLE MALLOW SALAD

1/2 C. whipping cream

1/4 C. mayonnaise or salad
  dressing

8 oz. cream cheese, softened

2 C. miniature marshmallows

8 oz. can pineapple tidbits or
  crushed pineapple, drained

1 medium cantaloupe or
  honeydew melon

Beat whipping cream until stiff peaks form; add mayonnaise and cream cheese and mix until smooth. Stir in marshmallows and pineapple and refrigerate at least 2 hours or overnight. Cut melon into 8 wedges and spoon about 1/2 cup of salad onto each.

**—BEST OF ALL B & B,
VALDEZ**

PINEAPPLE JELLO SALAD

1 6-oz. pkg. orange Jello

1 8-oz. can crushed pineapple

2 C. buttermilk

1/4 C. pecans, chopped
  (optional)

1 8-oz. carton whipped topping

Combine Jello and pineapple with its syrup in a large saucepan and bring to a boil, stirring constantly. Cool, stir in buttermilk and pecans. Turn into mold and chill. Serve with whipped topping.

**—WINDSOCK INN B & B,
JUNEAU**

PETITE PEA SALAD

1 pkg. frozen peas

1/4 lb. bacon, crisp fried

1 bunch green onions, chopped

1 C. celery, chopped

1 C. lite mayonnaise

1 C. cashews

Thaw peas. Crumble bacon. Combine chopped vegetables with mayonnaise, add bacon, fold in peas. Garnish with cashews. Serve chilled.

—ALL THE COMFORTS OF HOME, ANCHORAGE

ITALIAN PASTA SALAD

8 C. pasta, cooked

3 tomatoes, cubed

6 green onions, chopped

1 C. cheese, cubed (Cheddar, feta or mozzarella)

1/2 C. olives, chopped

6 oz. salami, chopped

green pepper or celery, chopped

Dressing:

olive oil

wine vinegar

garlic

Italian seasoning

salt and pepper

Combine all ingredients in salad bowl. Make dressing using proportions according to your own taste. Toss salad with dressing and serve.

—KROTO KREEK LODGE, BIG LAKE

TANANA SALMON SALAD

fresh or frozen salmon, cooked

lemon juice

light mayonnaise

lemon pepper

Yoshida sauce

parsley, onions, carrots and
   celery, finely chopped

Mix together in proportions according to size of salmon and personal taste. Serve with homemade rye bread, tomato slices and alfalfa sprouts.

**—TOLOVANA LODGE,
NENANA**

SPINACH–MUSHROOM SALAD

Salad:

1 lb. fresh spinach, torn

2/3 C. fresh mushrooms, sliced

1/2 C. bacon, cooked and
   crumbled (optional)

2 hard-cooked eggs, chopped

Mustard dressing:

2 T. Dijon mustard

1/4 C. vegetable oil

1 egg, slightly beaten

2 T. lemon juice

1 T. Parmesan cheese, grated

1 t. sugar

1 t. Worcestershire sauce

Combine dressing ingredients; toss dressing with salad ingredients.

**—ILIASKA LODGE,
ILIAMNA LAKE**

SPINACH SALAD DENALI

1 lb. spinach

1/2 C. green onions, sliced

1/3 C. warm bacon grease

Egg-Mustard Sauce:

3 hard-cooked egg yolks, mashed

1 1/2 t. mustard

1/2 C. cider vinegar

3 T. sugar

Toppings:

sliced almonds

3 hard cooked egg whites

4 slices cooked bacon, crumbled

mushrooms

Romano cheese

Egg-Mustard sauce: Mix egg yolks with rest of sauce ingredients until smooth.

Mix spinach (or substitute romaine lettuce) and green onions with warm bacon grease. Toss with sauce. and add toppings.

**—DENALI WEST LODGE,
LAKE MINCHUMINA**

SHRIMP SALAD

12 oz. seashell macaroni

1/2 lb. small shrimp, cooked

1/2 C. onions, chopped

1 C. celery, diced

2 tomatoes, seeded and diced

1/2 green pepper, seeded and diced

2 dozen snow peas, cut in 1-inch pieces

2 C. mayonnaise

2 T. fennel, chopped

2 t. dill, chopped

1/2 t. white pepper

1/2 t. salt

Cook macaroni according to package directions; drain and cool.

Combine shrimp and vegetables with macaroni in large bowl. Blend mayonnaise, herbs and seasonings together; stir into macaroni mixture. Chill well before serving. Serves 12.

—GLACIER BAY COUNTRY INN, GUSTAVUS

SUSHI-RICE SALAD

1 egg

2 C. uncooked white rice, rinsed
well

3 C. water, boiling

2 T. sherry or mirin

6 T. rice vinegar

1/2 C. sugar

1 1/4 t. salt

5 T. vegetable oil

1 carrot, minced

1 cucumber, peeled, seeded,
minced

2 scallions, all parts minced

1 1/2 C. peas, fresh or frozen,
lightly steamed

1/2 C. green beans, steamed

1/2 C. snow peas, steamed

1 yellow summer squash, minced
and lightly steamed

3 to 4 T. sushi pickled ginger
(amazu shoga), minced

1/2 red pepper, minced

Beat egg and pour into non-stick frying pan. Cook quickly over medium heat, swirling pan to distribute egg (do not stir), until egg is cooked through. Turn out onto plate and cool. Cut into 1/2-inch wide strips and set aside.

Cook rice in water 12 minutes covered, then let sit uncovered for 10 minutes.

Gently stir cooked egg and all remaining ingredients into rice. Serve at room temperature. Serves 8.

**—RIVERSONG LODGE,
YENTNA RIVER**

TOLOVANA SPECIAL SALAD

6 C. spiral multi-colored
  macaroni, cooked
several carrots, peeled & thinly
  sliced
several celery stalks, thinly sliced
1 C. garbanzo beans, cooked
2 C. sliced olives, black or green
1/2 C. sesame seeds
3/4 C. fresh parsley, chopped
1 pkg. tofu, cubed, or marinated
  artichoke hearts
virgin olive oil
lemon juice to taste
lemon pepper seasoning
red leaf lettuce

Mix all ingredients together and serve on a bed of red leaf lettuce.

—TOLOVANA LODGE, NENANA

OTHER VEGETABLES

ASPARAGUS PUFF

1 lb. asparagus

4 T. butter

2 T. onions, chopped

1/2 t. sugar

1 t. salt

2 T. water

6 eggs

1/3 C. heavy cream

fresh ground pepper

1 1/2 C. Muenster cheese,

grated

Cut asparagus into 1-inch pieces. Melt 2 tablespoons butter in a saute pan; saute onion until soft and golden. Add asparagus, sprinkle with sugar and 1/2 teaspoon salt, and toss for 1 minute. Add 2 tablespoons water, cover, steam cook for 1 to 2 minutes.

Remove cover and cool slightly. In separate bowl, beat together eggs, cream, 1/2 teaspoon salt and pepper to taste.

Melt 2 tablespoons butter in an oven-proof 10- x 10-inch baking dish. Pour in the egg mixture and cook over medium heat until the bottom is set (about 3 minutes). Arrange asparagus and onions in a single layer on top of the eggs. Bake at 425 degrees for 5 minutes. Remove from oven, cover asparagus with grated cheese, then bake an additional 10 minutes. Dish is done when the eggs have puffed and the cheese has lightly browned. Serves 4.

—RIVERSONG LODGE, YENTNA RIVER

BOBBIE'S BAKED BEANS

1/2 lb. bacon

1/2 large onion

1/2 green pepper

1 large can pork and beans

1/2 C. catsup

3/4 C. brown sugar

1/4 C. Worcestershire sauce

3/4 t. mustard

dash salt

Dice and saute bacon in a sauce pan. Chop onion and green pepper medium fine. Add to bacon and cook slightly. Pour off excess grease; add pork and beans. Stir and add remaining ingredients.

—QUIET PLACE LODGE B & B, HALIBUT COVE

BROCCOLI CASSEROLE

2 or 3 pkgs. frozen broccoli

1 can cream of mushroom soup

1 1/2 C. Cheddar cheese,
    shredded

garlic salt

dash pepper

paprika for garnish

Thaw broccoli and place in 9- x 13-inch pan. Mix soup and cheese together; add garlic salt and pepper to taste. Spread over broccoli. Sprinkle with paprika. Bake at 350 degrees for 30 minutes.

—BEAVER BEND B & B, FAIRBANKS

BROCCOLI CHEESE CASSEROLE

1 head of broccoli, cut into
  flowerettes

1/2 C. mayonnaise

1 can mushroom soup

1 T. lemon juice

1 C. sharp Cheddar, grated

1/2 C. cottage cheese

1 C. 1-inch cheese crackers,
  coarsely crushed

1/4 C. almonds, slivered

Place broccoli in greased 9- x 13-inch dish. Combine next 5 ingredients and pour over broccoli. Top with crushed crackers, cover and bake 30 minutes at 350 degrees. Garnish with almonds.

—ALL THE COMFORTS OF HOME, ANCHORAGE

CARROTS DENALI

1 1/2 lb. carrots

2 T. butter

2 t. dried tarragon

salt and pepper to taste

1/2 C. white wine

2 oz. brandy or Amaretto

Peel carrots, remove ends, cut into matchstick slices. Boil or steam until just crisp to the bite. Remove and plunge into cold water to stop cooking.

For final preparation add remaining ingredients to large frying pan and heat until ingredients boil. Add drained carrots, stirring until heated through. Remove from pan and serve. Serves 4.

—DENALI WILDERNESS LODGE DENALI PARK

SPICED CARROT STICKS

1 lb. carrots

3 T. water

2 T. salad oil

4 T. brown sugar

1 t. salt

1/4 t. dried mustard

1/4 t. cinnamon

1/8 t. ground ginger

Peel carrots and cut into sticks. Cook until tender-crisp; drain. Add remaining ingredients. Cover and refrigerate.

**—MEYERS CHUCK LODGE,
MEYERS CHUCK**

SPINACH CASSEROLE

2 pkgs. frozen chopped spinach,
    thawed and drained

2 C. cream-style cottage cheese

1/4 C. butter, cut into cubes

1 1/2 C. American cheese, cubed

3 eggs, beaten

1/4 C. flour

1 t. salt

Combine all ingredients. Pour into crock pot. Cover and cook on low for 4 to 5 hours.

**—DAYBREAK B & B,
FAIRBANKS**

TANGY GREEN BEANS

1 lb. fresh green beans,
   steamed and drained

3 T. salad oil

1 T. capers

1 t. salt

1/4 t. sugar

1/8 t. oregano

Combine all ingredients, cover and refrigerate. To serve, arrange beans on a plate lined with lettuce leaves.

**—MEYERS CHUCK LODGE,
MEYERS CHUCK**

ZUCCHINI CASSEROLE

6 C. zucchini, sliced

1 C. onion, chopped

1/2 C. green pepper, chopped

1 C. fresh mushrooms, chopped

butter

1 can cream of chicken soup

1 can cream of mushroom soup

1 C. sour cream

1 C. carrot, shredded

1 8-oz. pkg. herb seasoned
   stuffing cubes with seasoning
   packet

1/2 C. buttter, melted

Saute zucchini, onion, green pepper and mushrooms in butter. Spread in casserole dish. Mix soups, sour cream and shredded carrot together. Spoon this mixture over zucchini.

Mix stuffing cubes and seasoning packet; add melted butter and toss. Pour on top of zucchini. Bake at 350 degrees for 30 minutes.

**—DAYBREAK B & B,
FAIRBANKS**

CHAPTER 8

A Dab or a Dollop?

DRESSINGS

BLUE CHEESE SALAD DRESSING

1/4 lb. blue cheese

3 C. buttermilk

1/8 C. salt

1/4 T. garlic powder

1 qt. mayonnaise

Crumble blue cheese. Add buttermilk, salt and garlic. Mix well and add mayonnaise. Stir until smooth.

**—QUIET PLACE LODGE B & B,
HALIBUT COVE**

CINNAMON YOGURT DRESSING

1 C. plain yogurt

1 1/2 T. powdered sugar

1/4 t. cinnamon

1 T. fresh mint, finely chopped

Combine all ingredients, chill and serve with fresh fruit salads. (This dressing is good on grain cereals too!)

**—RIVERSONG LODGE,
YENTNA RIVER**

CURRANT DRESSING

1 C. sour cream

1 C. wild currant jelly

1 C. whipped cream

Mix ingredients well, chill, and spoon over a large bowl of fresh, chilled berries.

**—RIVERSONG LODGE,
YENTNA RIVER**

SAUCES & RELISHES

CREME FRAICHE

1 C. heavy cream

1 T. buttermilk

Combine cream and buttermilk in a jar. Cover tightly and shake for about 1 minute. Let stand at room temperature for at least 8 hours, or until thick.

—THE LILAC HOUSE B & B, ANCHORAGE

BARBECUE SAUCE

3/4 C. oil

1 t. paprika

1 T. prepared mustard

1 C. catsup

1 garlic clove, crushed

1/4 t. Tabasco sauce

1/4 C. butter, melted

1/4 C. lemon juice

1 T. brown sugar

1/4 t. pepper

1/2 t. Worcestershire sauce

Mix all ingredients. Use in any recipe calling for barbecue sauce.

—ALL THE COMFORTS OF HOME, ANCHORAGE

CRANBERRY-ONION SAUCE

1 can whole-berry cranberry
    sauce

1 pkg. dry onion soup mix

1 C. bottled Catalina salad
    dressing

Mix ingredients. Spread some sauce in bottom of baking pan. Add meat or fish of your choice—excellent with halibut, chicken or pork chops. Spread more sauce over the top. For halibut, bake at 350 degrees, covered, about 20 minutes, uncover and bake 20 minutes longer (meats will take longer).

—MEYERS CHUCK LODGE,
MEYERS CHUCK

FRESH SORREL SAUCE

1/4 C. dry vermouth

1/2 C. white wine

1/2 C. fish stock or chicken
    bouillon

2 shallots or 1/2 small onion,
    chopped

1/3 C. heavy cream

3 1/2 oz. fresh sorrel (see note)

4 T. unsalted butter

In a saucepan mix vermouth, wine, fish stock and shallots. Over medium heat, reduce to 1/4 cup. Add cream and reduce to half. Add sorrel. Whisk sauce, adding butter bit by bit. Place in double boiler and keep warm. Serve over halibut or salmon.

Note: If sorrel is not available, substitute 3 1/2 oz. chopped spinach and 1 T. lemon juice.

—MEYERS CHUCK LODGE,
MEYERS CHUCK

GINGERY RHUBARB CHUTNEY

2 lbs. red-skinned rhubarb,
   trimmed

1 1/2 C. onion, coarsely chopped

1 1/2 C. golden raisins

1 1/2 C. sugar

4 cloves garlic, peeled and
   minced

2 T. fresh ginger, finely minced

1 T. pickling or other fine non-
   iodized salt

2 t. mustard seed

1 t. ground allspice

1 t. ground coriander

1/2 t. dried red pepper flakes

1/4 t. ground cinnamon

1/4 t. ground cloves

2 C. cider vinegar

1/4 C. light corn syrup

Wash, drain and cut rhubarb into 1/2-inch dice (you should have 6 to 7 cups). Combine rhubarb with all the ingredients except the vinegar and corn syrup in a large pot; mix well. Bring to boiling over medium heat, lower the heat, partially cover the pot, and simmer the mixture, stirring it occasionally, until the onion pieces are translucent, about 30 minutes.

Add the vinegar and corn syrup and cook uncovered over medium-high heat, stirring almost constantly, until the chutney is thick enough to mound up slightly in a spoon, 20 to 30 minutes.

Ladle the boiling chutney into hot, clean half-pint or pint canning jars, leaving 1/4 inch of headspace. Seal the jars according to lid manufacturer's directions and process for 10 minutes in a boiling-water bath. Cool, label and store the jars for 3 weeks before opening. Makes 7 cups.

**—RIVERSONG LODGE,
YENTNA RIVER**

Highbush Cranberry Catsup

5 lbs. highbush cranberries
(see note)

2 1/2 C. cider vinegar

1 t. onion powder

6 C. sugar

1 T. salt

1 t. pepper

1 1/2 T. allspice

2 T. dried red pepper, chopped
(optional)

1 T. cloves

1 T. cinnamon

1 1/2 T. celery seed

Boil cranberries in at least 2 1/2 cups of water for 15 to 20 minutes. Strain through cheesecloth; use clear liquid for jelly. Place pulp in a large kettle, add vinegar, 1 1/2 cups more water, sugar and spices. Cook until thick. Pour into jars and seal. Process 20 minutes in boiling water bath.

Note: Substitute commercial cranberries if wild berries are not available.

—ILIASKA LODGE,
ILIAMNA LAKE

Shallot-Shrimp Sauce for Fish

1 T. unsalted butter, melted

2 1/2 t. shallots, minced

2 cloves garlic, crushed

1/4 t. saffron

1/4 C. dry white wine

1/2 C. small shrimp

6 T. whipping cream

Saute shallots, garlic and saffron in melted butter for 3 to 5 minutes. Add wine, shrimp and cream. Cook, reducing the sauce by half. Serve over hot fish. Extra good with halibut! Makes 2 portions.

—BARANOF WILDERNESS
LODGE, AUKE BAY

SWEET AND HOT RED PEPPER AND ONION RELISH

7 C. green or red (sweet)
   peppers

1/2 to 1 C. (to taste) hot
   peppers

2 T. salt

2 C. onions, finely diced

4 C. cider vinegar

3 C. sugar

2 C. light corn syrup

Core, derib and seed peppers; chop green or red peppers coarsely and finely chop hot peppers. Combine with salt in a pottery or stainless steel bowl; mix peppers well and let stand 3 hours.

Scrape the peppers and their liquid into a large pot. Add the onions, vinegar, sugar, and corn syrup. Bring the mixture to a boil over medium-high heat. Adjust the heat and cook, uncovered, at a moderate boil, stirring it often, until the peppers and onions are translucent and the syrup is thick, about 45 minutes.

Ladle the hot relish into hot, clean half-pint canning jars, leaving 1/4 inch headspace. Seal the jars with new 2-piece canning lids according to manufacturer's directions and process for 10 minutes in a boiling-water bath. Cool, label, and store the jars. Let the relish mellow for a few weeks, if possible, before serving it. Makes 7 cups.

**—RIVERSONG LODGE,
YENTNA RIVER**

VERY AMERICAN CRANBERRY SAUCE

1 1/2 C. pure maple syrup

1/2 C. water

1 t. ginger

4 C. fresh cranberries

Bring syrup, water and ginger to boil in a large, heavy saucepan over medium heat. Stir in cranberries. Simmer until berries begin to pop, about 5 minutes. Turn into a bowl and let cool. Spread on hot buttered cornbread. Makes 4 cups.

—RIVERSONG LODGE,
YENTNA RIVER

J E L L I E S & J A M S

FROZEN RHUBARB JAM

9 cups rhubarb, cut up

4 to 5 cups sugar

2 pkg. strawberry Jello (see note)

Mix rhubarb and sugar and let stand overnight.

Next morning cook for 4 minutes or until mixture boils.

Add Jello. Mix well and put in clean, steamed pint jars. Leave room for jam to expand. Freeze.

Note: This is also great when made with raspberry Jello, or try your favorite flavor.

—ARCTIC TERN B & B,
SOLDOTNA

ORANGE MARMALADE

3 medium oranges and 2
  medium lemons (3 C. total)

1/8 t. baking soda

5 C. sugar

1/2 bottle Certo fruit pectin

Remove peels in quarters from oranges and lemons. Lay peel flat; shave off and discard half of white part. Slice remaining peel very thin, or chop or grind. Add 1 1/2 cups water and the soda to rind; bring the mixture to a boil and simmer, covered, 20 minutes, stirring occasionally. Section or chop the peeled fruit; discard the seeds. Add this pulp and juice to the undrained, cooked rind. Simmer covered, for 10 minutes longer.

Make Marmalade: Measure 3 cups fruit mixture into a very large saucepan. Add sugar and mix well. Place over high heat, bring to a rolling boil and boil hard for 1 minute, stirring constantly. Remove from heat; at once stir in Certo. Skim off foam with metal spoon. Stir and skim for 7 minutes to cool slightly and to prevent floating fruit. Ladle into pre-sterilized jars, adjust lids and process in boiling water for 5 minutes. Makes about 7 jars.

**—FAVORITE BAY INN,
ANGOON**

BLUE-BARB JAM

3 C. rhubarb, finely cut

3 C. blueberries, crushed

1 C. sugar

1 bottle pectin

Simmer rhubarb and berries until rhubarb is tender. Mix in sugar. Boil hard 1 minute. Take off heat. Add pectin and stir 5 minutes. Pour into jars and seal. Makes 9 half-pint jars.

**—ARCTIC TERN B & B,
SOLDOTNA**

S Y R U P S

BLUE-BARB SYRUP

*2 qts. combined blueberries and
 rhubarb*

4 C. sugar

3/4 C. cold water

Mash fruit, sprinkle with sugar and let stand overnight. Add water, bring slowly to a boil and cook 20 minutes. Force through a double thickness of cheesecloth. Bring to a boil again and fill small, sterile glass jars or bottles. Adjust covers and seal. Use as a foundation for beverages, ices or saucesor on pancakes and waffles.

**—SELDOVIA ROWING CLUB
INN, SELDOVIA**

ROSE SYRUP

2 C. rose petals, washed

2 C. water

1 C. sugar

2 whole cloves

Put rose petals into a saucepan; cover with water. Add sugar and cloves. Bring to a boil, cover and simmer gently for 1 hour, or until the syrup is thick. If you want the syrup to be pinker, add a few drops of beet juice. Strain through a sieve and pour into bottles. This is good in hot tea.

**—RIVERSONG LODGE,
ANCHORAGE**

BUTTERS

FRESH STRAWBERRY BUTTER

1 C. fresh strawberries, pureed

1/2 lb. (2 cubes) butter, room
temperature

2 T. powdered sugar

Mix strawberry puree into butter in a food processor or with an electric mixer. When fairly smooth beat in sugar. Pack into a pretty box or mold and chill until serving time.

—FRANCINE'S B & B,
HOMER

HONEY-BERRY BUTTER

1/2 C. fresh blueberries, minced

1/2 C. butter, room temperature

1/3 C. honey

1/4 t. vanilla extract

A food processor works best for this recipe, but an electric blender will work also—but it is harder to scrape clean. Blot the berries on a paper towel so they are not so moist. Add all ingredients to the blender and process until creamy. Put the mixture into a bowl, cover and refrigerate. Let stand at room temperature before serving.

This also works well with strawberries and is good on any breakfast bread. Makes 3/4 cup.

—RIVERSONG LODGE,
YENTNA RIVER

— CHAPTER 9 —

Live A Little!

CAKES & CHEESECAKES

AMISH ZUCCHINI CAKE

4 eggs

2 C. sugar

1 C. vegetable oil

2 C. flour

2 t. cinnamon

2 t. baking powder

1 t. baking soda

1 t. salt

1 C. crushed pineapple, well
   drained

1/2 C. pecans, chopped

2 C. raw zucchini, grated
   (squeeze out excess water)

2 t. vanilla

1 t. butter flavoring

In large bowl of electric mixer, mix eggs and sugar until lemon colored. Add oil and mix well; add flour, cinnamon, baking powder, baking soda, and salt. Beat well for 2 minutes. Stir in pineapple, nuts, zucchini (squeeze between paper towels to remove excess moisture), vanilla and butter flavor. Mix thoroughly.

Pour into well buttered and floured 10-inch tube pan. Bake at 350 degrees for 1 hour and 20 minutes. Cool on rack for 30 minutes before removing from pan. Glaze while warm if desired.

**—WASILLA LAKE B & B,
WASILLA**

BEV'S KILLER CUPCAKES

4 oz. semisweet chocolate

1 t. vanilla

1 C. butter

4 eggs

1 1/2 C. sugar

1 C. flour

Filling:

8 oz. cream cheese, softened

1/4 C. sugar

1 egg

dash of salt

3/4 C. semisweet chocolate chips

Melt chocolate, vanilla and butter. Set aside. Beat eggs until thick, add sugar. Beat in the flour. Fold in the butter and chocolate mix. Spoon into greased tins 2/3 full.

Filling: Mix cream cheese, sugar, eggs and salt until blended. Stir in chocolate chips. Drop a heaping teaspoon of filling onto each cupcake. Bake at 350 degrees for 30 minutes. Makes about 20 cupcakes.

**—WALLIN'S HILLTOP B & B,
ANCHOR POINT**

CARAMEL-NUT PUDDING CAKE

1 C. Bisquick

1/2 C. brown sugar, firmly packed

1/2 C. raisins, if desired

1/2 C. nuts, chopped

1/2 C. milk

Brown sugar topping:

1 C. brown sugar, firmly packed

1 T. butter or margarine

2 C. boiling water

Lightly grease an 8-inch square pan. In a medium bowl, combine Bisquick, brown sugar, raisins (if desired), and nuts. Mix well. Add milk and blend well. Pour into prepared pan.

Brown sugar topping: In a small bowl, mix brown sugar, butter or margarine and boiling water. Gently pour over top of cake without stirring. Bake at 375 degrees 30 to 40 minutes, until cake springs back when lightly touched. Cool 15 minutes before serving.

—MEYERS CHUCK LODGE,
MEYERS CHUCK

CARROT CAKE

2 C. sugar

1 1/2 C. oil

4 eggs

1 1/2 C. flour

2 t. baking soda

1 1/2 t. baking powder

1 t. cinnamon

1 t. allspice

dash of cloves

3 C. grated carrots

Combine sugar, oil and eggs; mix thoroughly. Add dry ingredients and stir well. Stir in carrots. Pour into greased and floured 13- x 9-inch pan. Bake at 325 degrees for 40 minutes.

—ALL THE COMFORTS OF
HOME, ANCHORAGE

CHOCOLATE ZUCCHINI CAKE

1/2 C. butter

1/2 C. oil

1 3/4 C. sugar

2 eggs

1/2 C. sour milk or buttermilk

1 1/2 t. vanilla

1/2 t. cinnamon

1/2 t. cloves

2 1/2 C. flour (use white, whole
    wheat or a combination)

1 t. soda

4 T. cocoa

1/2 t. salt

1 to 3 C. zucchini, shredded
    (squeeze out excess water)

Frosting:

1 lb. powdered sugar

1/2 C. butter

1/2 C. cocoa

1/2 C. nuts, chopped

1 t. vanilla

milk

Combine butter, oil, and sugar. Beat eggs and mix well with sugar mixture. Beat in milk, vanilla and spices. Sift together remaining dry ingredients; add to wet. Stir in zucchini. Pour into a greased and floured 13- x 9-inch pan. Bake 30 minutes at 350 degrees.

Frosting: Combine frosting ingredients, adding enough milk to make spreading consistency. Frost cake while warm.

**—TOLOVANA LODGE,
NENANA**

DENALI WEST SPECIAL

1/2 C. flour

1/4 C. cocoa

1/2 T. baking powder

4 egg yolks

3/4 C. sugar

1 t. vanilla

1/4 t. almond flavoring

2 T. water

4 egg whites

Chocolate Mousse Filling:

3/4 C. butter

3/4 C. powdered sugar

6 egg yolks

2 C. semi-sweet chocolate pieces,
    melted and cooled

1/4 t. almond flavoring

6 egg whites

Garnish:

sweetened whipped cream

chocolate curls

sliced almonds

Sift together flour, cocoa and baking powder; set aside. Beat egg yolks until thick and pale yellow. Gradually stir in sugar.

Add vanilla, almond flavoring and water. Fold this mixture into dry ingredients. Beat egg whites until stiff, glossy peaks form. Fold into batter.

Spread batter in greased and floured 15- x 10-inch jellyroll pan; bake at 375 degrees for 12 minutes. Loosen cake and invert onto clean dishtowel sprinkled with powdered sugar. Roll up from short end; cool.

Chocolate Mousse Filling:
Beat butter and sugar together on high speed until fluffy. Add egg yolks and beat 5 minutes on medium speed. Add melted chocolate and flavoring and beat until mixed thoroughly. Beat egg whites until soft peaks form; fold into chocolate mixture. Refrigerate 1 hour.

Unroll cake and remove towel. Spread with filling and reroll. Pipe or spread sweetened whipped cream on cake and garnish with chocolate curls and sliced almonds. Serves 10.

—DENALI WEST LODGE,
LAKE MINCHUMINA

FRESH RHUBARB CAKE

1 1/2 C. brown sugar

1/2 C. shortening

1 egg

1 tsp. vanilla

2 C. flour

1 t. soda

1/4 t. salt

1 C. sour milk or buttermilk

1/2 C. nuts, chopped

1 1/2 C. rhubarb, in small pieces

1/4 C. sugar

1/2 t. cinnamon

Cream brown sugar and shortening; stir in egg and vanilla. Sift together flour, soda and salt and add alternately with buttermilk, mixing well. Pour batter into a greased and floured 9- x 13-inch pan. Mix sugar and cinnamon and sprinkle over top. Bake at 350 degrees for 35 to 40 minutes. (Note: this also makes a delicious coffeecake.)

—**SUNRISE B & B,
STERLING**

GOLDEN DELICIOUS APPLE WALNUT CAKE

2 C. flour

2 t. baking soda

2 t. cinnamon

1 t. salt

2 C. sugar

4 C. apple, chopped

1 C. black walnuts, chopped

2 eggs

1/2 C. vegetable oil

2 t. vanilla

Lemon Butter Frosting:

1/3 C. butter, softened

3 C. powdered sugar

1 egg yolk, beaten

3 T. lemon juice

1 1/2 T. lemon rind, grated

Sift together flour, baking soda, cinnamon and salt. Combine sugar, chopped apple and chopped walnuts. Beat together the eggs, oil and vanilla. Add flour and apple mixture alternately to egg mixture. Pour into greased and floured 9- x 13-inch pan. Bake at 350 degrees for 1 hour. Cool and frost.

Lemon Butter Frosting:
Combine butter and sugar. Blend in egg yolk. Add lemon juice and rind and blend thoroughly.

—**ARCTIC TERN B & B,
SOLDOTNA**

HOT FUDGE PUDDING CAKE

1 1/2 C. Bisquick

1/2 C. sugar

2 T. cocoa

3/4 C. chopped nuts

1/2 C. milk

1 t. vanilla

3/4 C. brown sugar, firmly
   packed

1/4 C. cocoa

1 1/2 C. boiling water

In an ungreased, 8-inch square pan, combine Bisquick, sugar, 2 tablespoons cocoa, nuts, milk and vanilla. Mix well. Combine brown sugar and 1/4 cup cocoa in a small bowl. Sprinkle over top of cake mixture. Gently pour boiling water over top. Do not stir. Bake at 350 degrees 35 to 40 minutes, until edges separate from pan. Cool before serving.

**—MEYERS CHUCK LODGE,
MEYERS CHUCK**

HOT MILK SPONGE CAKE

2 C. flour

1 t. baking powder

1 t. salt

1 C. milk

4 T. butter

4 eggs

2 C. sugar

2 t. vanilla

Sift flour, baking powder and salt together. Heat milk and butter until butter melts. Beat eggs and sugar on high speed for 8 to 10 minutes; add vanilla. Combine all ingredients and mix briefly. Bake at 350 degrees, 25 to 30 minutes for 9-inch rounds; 55 to 60 minutes for a tube pan.

**—ARCTIC TERN B & B,
SOLDOTNA**

Grease and flour bottoms of 2 9-inch round cake pans or sides and center of tube pan.

OATMEAL CAKE

1 1/2 C. boiling water

1/2 C. butter or margarine

1 C. quick-cooking oats

1 C. sugar

2 eggs

1 C. brown sugar

1 1/2 C. flour

1 t. soda

1/2 t. salt

1 1/2 t. vanilla

Frosting:

1/2 C. butter or margarine

1 C. sugar

1/2 C. evaporated milk

2 t. vanilla

1 C. coconut, chopped

1 C. nuts, chopped

Pour boiling water over oats and butter. Stir, cover and let stand 20 minutes. Add white sugar, eggs and brown sugar; mix well. Stir in remaining ingredients, mix well and pour into a greased and floured 9- x 13-inch pan. Bake 30 to 35 minutes at 350 degrees or until pick inserted in center of cake comes out clean.

Frosting: Mix the first 4 frosting ingredients together in a saucepan and cook over medium heat until mixture boils. Continue boiling for 5 minutes, stirring often. Add coconut and nuts (we use walnuts). Spread on warm cake. Put under the broiler until golden brown. This cake keeps very well—the flavor improves every day.

—KROTO CREEK LODGE,
BIG LAKE

PARSON'S DELIGHT

*1 pkg. Duncan Hines Golden
   Butter cake mix*

1/2 C. water

4 eggs

*1 3 oz. pkg. instant vanilla
   pudding mix*

*1 4 oz. pkg. German's
   chocolate, grated*

1 6 oz. pkg. chocolate chips

1/2 C. vegetable oil

1 C. sour cream

Glaze:

1 C. powdered sugar

2 to 3 T. milk

1 t. vanilla

Combine cake mix with water and eggs in large mixing bowl; beat well. Stir in pudding mix, grated chocolate, chocolate chips, oil and sour cream. Mix thoroughly; pour into greased bundt pan. Bake at 350 degrees for 50 to 55 minutes. Cool 20 minutes.

Glaze: Combine ingredients and mix until smooth. When cake has cooled, removed from pan and glaze.

**—NORTHWOODS LODGE,
EAGLE RIVER**

RHUBARB CAKE

2 C. sugar

1/2 C. shortening

1 egg

1 C. buttermilk or sour milk

2 C. flour

1 t. soda

2 C. rhubarb, finely chopped
   and lightly floured

1 t. vanilla

Topping:

1/4 C. sugar

1/4 C. margarine

2 T. flour

1 t. cinnamon

Cream together sugar and shortening. Stir in egg. Mix flour and soda; add alternately with buttermilk to sugar-shortening mixture. Mix well. Add rhubarb and vanilla. Pour into greased and floured 9- x 13-inch pan.

Topping: Mix ingredients until crumbly, then sprinkle over cake. Bake at 350 degrees for 1 hour.

**—WALLIN'S HILLTOP B & B,
ANCHOR POINT**

RHUBARB PUDDING CAKE

4 C. diced rhubarb

1 C. sugar

3/4 C. water

1/4 C. shortening

1/2 C. sugar

1 egg

1/2 t. vanilla

1 C. flour

2 t. baking powder

1/4 t. salt

1/2 C. milk

Cook rhubarb, 1 cup sugar and water until rhubarb is tender; keep hot. Cream shortening and 1/2 cup sugar; beat in egg and vanilla. Sift together flour, baking powder and salt; add alternately with milk to creamed mixture. Pour batter into greased 2-quart glass dish. Spoon hot rhubarb sauce over batter. Bake at 350 degrees for 40 minutes. Serves 6.

—ANCHOR RIVER B & B, ANCHOR POINT

QUICK POPPY SEED CAKE

1 box yellow cake mix

4 eggs

1 C. water

1 t. almond extract

1/3 C. oil

1 3 oz. pkg. vanilla pudding mix

1/2 C. poppy seeds

powdered sugar

fresh strawberries, sliced

fresh kiwi slices

fresh banana slices

Combine ingredients. Bake 50 minutes at 350 degrees in heavily buttered bundt pan. Cool, then invert onto plate.

Sprinkle cake with powdered sugar and garnish with fresh fruit slices.

—ALL THE COMFORTS OF HOME, ANCHORAGE

WHOLE WHEAT CARROT CAKE

1 C. cooking oil

1 C. sugar

1 C. brown sugar

1 t. vanilla

4 eggs

2 C. whole wheat flour

1 t. salt

1/3 C. nonfat dry milk

1 t. baking soda

1 t. baking powder

2 t. cinnamon

3 C. carrots, shredded

1 C. walnuts, chopped

powdered sugar

Blend oil and sugars with mixer on low speed until combined. Add vanilla. Beat in the eggs one at a time, beating well after each addition. In another bowl, stir together the dry ingredients. Add to the egg mixture and mix until well blended. Stir in carrots and walnuts by hand. Pour the batter into a greased and floured 10-inch tube or 12-cup bundt pan. Bake at 350 degrees for 50 to 60 minutes or until wooden pick inserted in center comes out clean. Cool in pan; invert onto serving plate. Sprinkle sifted powdered sugar on top. Serves 10 to 12.

**—GLACIER BAY COUNTRY INN,
GUSTAVUS**

Chocolate "Moose" Cheesecake

Crust:

1/2 C. butter, softened

1 1/2 C. chocolate wafer
   cookies, crushed

1/4 C. brown sugar

Cake:

2 lbs. cream cheese

8 eggs

pinch salt

juice of 1 lemon

1 1/4 C. sugar

4 oz. semisweet baking
   chocolate, melted

4 oz. chocolate liqueur

Crust: Thoroughly mix butter with remaining crust ingredients. When mixed, layer bottom of 10-inch springform pan with crust, being careful to evenly layer crust in pan.

Cake: Have cream cheese at room temperature (about 70 degrees). Beat cream cheese in mixing bowl until completely smooth. Add eggs one at a time, mix until smooth. Continue to mix, adding salt, lemon juice, sugar, melted chocolate and liqueur. When mixture is smooth and thoroughly combined, pour over crust in springform pan.

Bake at 350 degrees for 60 minutes. After 60 minutes, open oven door to reduce heat for about 5 minutes, turn temperature down to 200 degrees and continue to bake for 20 minutes. Remove from oven; cool on rack, then refrigerate before serving.

**—DENALI WILDERNESS LODGE,
DENALI PARK**

MICROWAVE ORANGE CHEESECAKE

Crust:

3 T. butter or margarine

2/3 C. graham crackers, finely
  crushed

1 T. sugar

Cheesecake:

2 3-oz. pkgs. cream cheese

1 beaten egg

1/3 C. sugar

1/3 C. dairy sour cream

1 t. finely shredded orange peel

3 T. orange juice

1/4 t. vanilla

1/4 C. orange marmalade

Crust: In a microwave-safe pie plate melt butter or margarine at 100 percent power (high) in microwave (45 to 60 seconds). Add crushed graham crackers and 1 tablespoon sugar; stir until moistened. Press mixture firmly against bottom and sides of pie plate. Microwave, uncovered, on high for 1 to 1 1/2 minutes or until set, giving pie plate a half-turn after 30 seconds. Set aside.

Cheesecake: In a microwave-safe mixing bowl cook cream cheese, uncovered, on 50 percent power (medium) for 1 to 1 1/2 minutes or until softened. Add beaten egg, 1/3 cup sugar, and sour cream and stir until smooth. Add orange peel, orange juice, and vanilla. Mix well. Pour mixture into crust. Cook, uncovered, on medium for 8 to 10 minutes or until a knife inserted 1 inch from edge comes out clean, giving pie plate a quarter-turn every 2 minutes. (Center will be slightly set but not firm). Cool slightly.

Meanwhile, in a small microwave-safe bowl or custard cup, heat orange marmalade on high for 30 to 60 seconds or until warm. Spoon over top of cheesecake. Refrigerate at least 3 hours or until set. Makes 6 servings.

**—KACHEMAK BAY
WILDERNESS LODGE,
CHINA POOT BAY**

PRALINE CHEESECAKE

Crust:

1 1/4 C. graham cracker crumbs

1/4 C. sugar

1/4 C. pecans, chopped

1/4 C. butter, melted

Cheesecake:

8 oz. cream cheese

1 C. brown sugar

1/2 C. evaporated milk

2 T. flour

1 1/2 t. vanilla

3 eggs

1 C. pecan halves, roasted

Praline Sauce:

1 C. dark corn syrup

1/4 C. cornstarch

2 T. brown sugar

1 t. vanilla

Crust: Combine the graham cracker crumbs, sugar and pecans in a small bowl. Stir in the butter. Press crumb mixture over the bottom and 2 inches up the sides of a 9-inch springform pan. Bake at 350 degrees for 10 minutes.

Cheesecake: Beat the cream cheese, brown sugar, milk, flour and vanilla together well in a medium bowl. Add eggs, continuing to beat just until blended. Pour the mixture into the graham cracker crust. Bake at 350 degrees for 1 hour or until set. Cool in the pan 30 minutes before removing rim. Cool completely, then arrange pecan halves on top of the cheesecake.

Praline Sauce: Combine corn syrup, cornstarch and brown sugar in a small saucepan. Cook until thick and bubbly. Remove from heat and stir in vanilla. Cool slightly. Pour the warm sauce over individual slices of cheesecake. Makes 10 to 12 servings.

—RIVERSONG LODGE,
YENTNA RIVER

C O O K I E S

AMISH SUGAR COOKIES

1 C. sugar

1 C. powdered sugar

1 C. butter, softened

2 eggs

1 C. oil

1 t. vanilla

1/4 t. salt

1 t. soda

4 C. flour

1 t. cream of tartar

Cream together sugar, powdered sugar and butter. Add eggs, oil and vanilla and mix well. Sift dry ingredients together and add.

Form into balls and press with sugared glass. Bake at 350 degrees for 8 to 10 minutes.

**—DAYBREAK B & B,
FAIRBANKS**

CHOCOLATE CHIP OATMEAL COOKIES

2 C. light brown sugar

2 C. margarine

3 eggs

1 1/2 t. vanilla

1 pkg. (large size) instant vanilla
   pudding mix

2 C. flour

2 t. baking soda

6 1/2 C. quick-cooking oats

12 oz. chocolate chips

Mix brown sugar, margarine, eggs, vanilla and pudding mix. Add flour and baking soda and mix well. Stir in oats and chocolate chips. Drop batter by teaspoonfuls onto greased cookie sheets; bake at 375 degrees 8 to 10 minutes or until brown. Yield: 8 dozen.

**—WINDSOCK INN,
DOUGLAS**

CRANBERRY DROP COOKIES

1 C. sugar

3/4 C. brown sugar. packed

1/2 C. margarine or butter,
  softened

1/4 C. milk

2 T. orange juice

1 egg

3 C. flour

1 t. baking powder

1/2 t. salt

1/4 t. baking soda

2 1/2 cups fresh or frozen
  cranberries, coarsely chopped

1 C. nuts, chopped

Preheat the oven to 375 degrees. Mix sugars and margarine. Stir in milk, orange juice and egg. Sift together flour, baking powder, salt and baking soda; add to batter. Mix in cranberries and nuts. Drop by rounded teaspoonfuls onto greased cookie sheets. Bake 10 to 15 minutes. Makes 5 dozen cookies.

**—RIVERSONG LODGE,
YENTNA RIVER**

GRAMMA MARQUARDT'S CHOCOLATE CHIP COOKIES

1 C. butter

3/4 C. brown sugar

3/4 C. sugar

2 eggs, beaten

1 t. baking soda

1 t. hot water

1 t. vanilla

2 3/4 C. flour

1 t. salt

1 C. nuts

12 oz. semisweet chocolate chips

Combine butter, sugars and beaten eggs. Dissolve soda in water. Add to egg mixture; stir in vanilla. Add flour, salt, nuts and chips. Bake on greased baking sheet at 375 degrees for 10 to 12 minutes.

—ALL THE COMFORTS OF HOME, ANCHORAGE

"GUIDE" COOKIES

1 1/3 C. shortening

1 1/3 C. butter

2 C. sugar

2 C. brown sugar

4 eggs

6 C. flour

2 t. salt

4 t. vanilla

2 t. baking soda

2 C. nuts, chopped

24 oz. semisweet chocolate chips

Mix first 4 ingredients until smooth. Add eggs 2 at a time, mixing well. Add flour, salt, vanilla and soda. Mix well. Add nuts and chips. Drop by teaspoonfuls onto ungreased cookie sheets; bake at 375 degrees 8 minutes. Cookies will not look done and will not be browned, but will finish cooking while cooling. Makes 20 dozen.

—ILIASKA LODGE, ILIAMNA LAKE

HAZEL MUSSER'S SUGAR COOKIES

2 C. sugar

1 C. shortening

2 eggs

1 C. buttermilk

1 t. baking soda

1 t. salt

2 T. baking powder

1 t. vanilla

flour

Cream sugar and shortening; add eggs and beat well. Add soda to buttermilk, then stir into sugar, shortening and egg mixture. Add salt, baking powder, vanilla and enough flour to form a dough that will not stick to the board. Roll out, cut and bake at 350 degrees for 8 minutes. Makes about 3 1/2 dozen.

Hazel Musser's farm was up the road from my folks' farm back in Michigan, and she shared this recipe with my mother. A favorite memory is my sister and me coming home from school, sitting at the kitchen table with Mom and Grandma and eating these cookies with butter spread on them while we drank a cup of tea and talked about our school day. I still enjoy the cookies served that way, but I also frost them sometimes.

—MARLOW'S KENAI RIVER B & B, SOLDOTNA

MINT CHOCOLATE CHIP COOKIES

3/4 C. butter

1/2 C. sugar

1/2 C. brown sugar

1 egg

1 t. vanilla extract

1 t. peppermint extract

1 1/2 C. flour

1/4 C. cocoa

1 t. baking soda

1/4 t. salt

1 C. semisweet chocolate chips

Cream butter and sugars; beat in egg. Add remaining ingredients and mix well. Drop by teaspoonfuls onto greased cookie sheet and bake at 350 degrees for 12 to 15 minutes. Makes 2 1/2 dozen irresistible cookies.

**—RIVERSONG LODGE,
YENTNA RIVER**

New Brunswick Coffee Squares

1 1/2 C. flour

1/2 t. salt

1/2 t. baking powder

1/2 C. butter

1 C. brown sugar

1 egg

1 t. vanilla

1/2 C. cold, brewed coffee

Icing:

1 1/2 C. powdered sugar

1 T. cocoa

1/4 C. butter, melted

salt

1/2 t. vanilla

Sift together flour, salt, and baking powder. Set aside. Cream butter and brown sugar. Beat in egg and vanilla. Add dry ingredients to mixture alternately with cold coffee. Pour into greased 8- x 8-inch pan and bake at 350 degrees for 30 minutes.

Icing: Mix icing ingredients with enough cold coffee to make spreading consistency.

—THE SUMMER INN B & B, HAINES

OATMEAL BREAKFAST COOKIES

6 strips bacon

2/3 C. margarine, softened

2/3 C. sugar

1 egg

1 t. vanilla

2/3 C. all purpose flour

1/2 t. baking powder

1/2 t. salt

1 C. shredded Cheddar cheese

1 1/2 C. oatmeal

1/2 C. wheat germ

Fry bacon until crisp; drain, crumble and set aside. Mix well margarine, sugar, egg and vanilla. Stir in flour, baking powder and salt. Add cheese, oatmeal, wheat germ and crumbled bacon. Drop by spoonfuls onto ungreased cookie sheet. Bake at 350 degrees for 12 to 14 minutes. Cool before removing from sheet.

**—ARCTIC TERN B & B,
SOLDOTNA**

P I E S

Fresh Strawberry Pie

2 C. flour

1/2 t. salt

3 T. sugar

3/4 C. oil

3 T. milk

1 C. sugar

3 T. cornstarch

pinch of salt

1 C. water

2 T. Karo syrup

3 T. strawberry Jello powder

2 pints fresh strawberries,
   washed and hulled

whipped cream

Combine flour, salt, sugar, oil and milk in 10-inch pie pan. Press and shape, then bake at 350 degrees for 20 minutes.

To make glaze, mix sugar, cornstarch and pinch of salt in saucepan; add water and Karo syrup. Boil until clear, then cool slightly and add Jello powder. Arrange strawberries in baked pie crust; pour glaze over. Chill 3 hours. Serve with whipped cream.

—CLAY'S QUALITY B & B, HOMER

PINEAPPLE CHEESE PIE

Crust:

4 C. corn flakes

2 T. sugar

4 T. butter, melted

Filling:

1 envelope unflavored gelatin

1/2 C. cold water

3 eggs, separated

1 can crushed pineapple, not
    drained

1 t. lemon rind, grated

2 T. lemon juice

3/4 C. sugar

1 C. cream-style cottage cheese

1/4 t. salt

Crust: Mix ingredients and press into 9-inch pie pan, reserving 3 tablespoons crumbs for topping. Chill thoroughly.

Filling: Add gelatin to cold water and set aside. Beat egg yolks slightly in double boiler or heavy saucepan. Add crushed pineapple, lemon rind and lemon juice and 1/4 cup sugar. Cook, stirring, until thick. Add gelatin mixture and stir until dissolved. Remove from heat. Force cottage cheese through wire strainer, add to hot mixture, cool until beginning to thicken. Beat egg whites with salt. When stiff, gradually beat in 1/2 cup sugar, and fold into pineapple-cheese mixture. Heap in chilled crust. Sprinkle with the reserved crumbs and chill at least 3 hours. Serves 6.

**—BETTY'S B & B,
FAIRBANKS**

RHUBARB CRISP PIE

pastry for 9-inch single-crust pie

4 C. rhubarb, sliced

3/4 C. flour

3/4 C. sugar

Topping:

1 1/2 C. oats

1/2 C. brown sugar

1/4 C. butter, melted

pinch of salt

Roll pastry out and fit into 9-inch pie pan. Fold edges under and flute decoratively.

Combine rhubarb, flour and sugar; pour into prepared crust. Mix topping ingredients until crumbly. Sprinkle over rhubarb mixture. Bake at 450 degrees 10 minutes; reduce temperature to 350 degrees and bake 30 to 35 minutes or until crust is golden and filling is bubbly.

**—GLACIER BAY COUNTRY INN,
GUSTAVUS**

GLACIER BAY RHUBARB CUSTARD PIE

pastry for 9-inch single crust pie

4 to 5 C. fresh rhubarb, cut
   into 1/2-inch pieces

2 C. sugar

1 C. flour

5 egg yolks

1/3 C. milk

Arrange rhubarb in pie shell. Blend sugar, flour, egg yolks and milk; pour over rhubarb. Bake at 450 degrees for 10 minutes; reduce temperature to 350 degrees and bake for 40 more minutes, or until filling is set and pastry is browned. Serves 8.

**—GLACIER BAY COUNTRY INN,
GUSTAVUS**

Roll out pastry and fit into 9-inch pie pan. Fold edges under and make a decorative rim.

ANCHOR RIVER RHUBARB CUSTARD PIE

1 1/4 C. sugar

1/4 C. flour

1/4 t. ground nutmeg

dash of salt

3 eggs

5 C. rhubarb, chopped

pastry for 9-inch lattice-top pie

2 T. butter

Mix sugar, flour, nutmeg, and salt. Add eggs; beat until smooth. Stir in rhubarb. Line pie plate with pastry. Fill with rhubarb mixture, dot with butter. Adjust lattice top and seal. Bake at 400 degrees for 50 minutes.

—ANCHOR RIVER B & B,
ANCHOR POINT

EVELYN RUSSELL'S NEVER-TURNED-DOWN APPLE PIE

Crust:

1 1/2 t. salt

3/4 C. shortening

3 C. flour

1/3 C. (about) cold water

Filling:

6 large Granny Smith apples, peeled, cored and sliced

1 T. cinnamon

1 C. sugar

Mix crust ingredients in food processor 10 seconds. Put in refrigerator.

Combine filling ingredients. Divide crust in half and roll out. Fit half into 10-inch pie pan; pour in filling. Add top crust and cut vents. Bake at 375 degrees for 45 minutes.

—RUSSELL'S B & B,
PALMER

SALMONBERRY PIE

Crust for 1 9-inch pie, pre-baked
   (plain pastry or graham
   cracker)

1 C. sugar

1 C. water

3 T. cornstarch

3 T. red Jello powder

4 C. fresh salmonberries

whipped cream

nutmeg

Place sugar, water, and cornstarch in saucepan. Cook over medium heat, stirring constantly, until clear. Add Jello and stir until dissolved. Gently fold in fresh salmonberries. Pour into baked pie shell and chill until firm. Top with whipped cream and dash of nutmeg.

—LION'S DEN WILDERNESS LODGE, KODIAK

WILDBERRY PIE

5 1/2 C. blueberries or
   salmonberries

1 C. sugar

3 T. flour

2 T. tapioca

butter

pastry for 2-crust pie

Mix first 4 ingredients and pour into unbaked 9- or 10-inch pie crust. Dot with butter; add top crust. Bake at 425 degrees for 20 minutes.

—LISIANSKI LODGE & CHARTERS, PELICAN

P U D D I N G S

PAT'S PLACE RICE PUDDING

1 qt. milk

1/4 C. raw rice

1 t. salt

1/3 C. sugar

2 T. margarine

dash of nutmeg

1 t. vanilla

Combine all ingredients and pour into a greased baking dish or casserole. Bake at 300 degrees for 2 1/2 hours, stirring frequently.

—PAT'S PLACE B & B,
WASILLA

MARLOW'S BREAD PUDDING

2 C. dry bread cubes

4 C. milk, scalded

3/4 C. sugar

1 T. butter

1/4 t. salt

4 eggs, slightly beaten

1 t. vanilla

1/2 C. seedless raisins

Soak bread in milk for 5 minutes. Add sugar, butter and salt. Pour slowly over eggs, add vanilla and mix well. Fold in raisins. Pour into greased 1 1/2-quart baking dish and bake at 350 degrees in pan of hot water for 1 hour. Serve warm.

Even though bread pudding is traditionally a dessert, my family has enjoyed it for breakfast for years, and my guests say they like it then, too.

—MARLOW'S KENAI RIVER
B & B, SOLDOTNA

MARY'S BREAD PUDDING

2 eggs, beaten

2 1/4 C. milk

1 t. vanilla

1/2 t. cinnamon

1/4 t. salt

2 C. day-old bread, cubed

1/4 C. brown sugar

1/2 C. raisins

Combine eggs, milk, vanilla, cinnamon and salt; stir in remaining ingredients. Pour into an 8-inch, round casserole. Place in larger shallow pan with 1 inch hot water. Bake at 350 degrees for 45 minutes or until knife inserted halfway between center and edge comes out clean. Serves 4 to 6. Recipe can be doubled but allow a longer baking time.

**—ANCHOR RIVER B & B,
ANCHOR POINT**

LEMON BREAD PUDDING

1 qt. nonfat milk

4 eggs

artificial sweetener to equal 16

   teaspoons sugar

2 t. vanilla

2 t. lemon extract

4 slices bread, cubed

dash nutmeg

Combine first 5 ingredients in blender and blend on low for 30 seconds. Divide the bread equally among 4 individual baking dishes. Pour on egg mixture, pushing bread down to soak. Sprinkle with nutmeg. Set baking dishes in a large pan of hot water; bake at 350 degrees for 35 minutes. Cool. Cover and refrigerate. Serves 4.

**—PAT'S PLACE B & B,
WASILLA**

OTHER DESSERTS

BAKED APPLES

4 crisp Granny Smith or

   Macintosh apples, washed

   and cored

Filling:

3 T. raisins

2 T. chopped walnuts

3 T. brown sugar

Topping:

butter

milk or half-and-half

Mix filling ingredients; fill apples with the mixture. Dot the tops of the filled apples with butter. Place in baking dish with 1 cup boiling water. Bake at 375 degrees for 45 minutes, basting once or twice with juices. Serve in individual bowls. Pour juice over the top and pass a pitcher of milk or half-and-half.

—**BLUEBERRY LODGE B & B,
DOUGLAS**

CHOCOLATE MINT FRANGOES

1 C. butter

2 C. powdered sugar

4 squares unsweetened

   chocolate, melted and cooled

4 eggs

1/3 t. peppermint extract

2 t. vanilla

Cream butter and powdered sugar. Beat until very light; add the chocolate and beat. Add eggs and flavorings and beat well. Spoon into foil baking cups and freeze. Serve with whipped cream.

—**TUTKA BAY LODGE,
HOMER**

MICROWAVE APPLE CRISP

6 C. peeled, cored and sliced
  cooking apples

2/3 C. quick-cooking oats

1/2 t. nutmeg

1/3 C. flour

1/2 t. cinnamon

3/4 C. brown sugar, packed

1/4 C. butter or margarine

Place apple slices in an 8- x 8-inch microwave-safe baking dish. Combine remaining ingredients, except butter, in medium mixing bowl. Cut in butter until crumbly. Sprinkle over apples. Microwave for 16 to 20 minutes on high or until apples are tender. Serves 6.

—ALASKAN FRONTIER GARDENS B & B, ANCHORAGE

GLORIOUS GOAT'S MILK CUSTARD

1/2 C. sugar

1 qt. goat's milk (cow's milk
  may be substituted)

3 egg yolks

1/4 C. milk

6 T. cornstarch

1 t. vanilla

1/4 t. salt

Place sugar in bottom of large saucepan. Slowly (to not disturb sugar) add milk. Don't stir. Bring to a boil.

While milk is heating, mix remaining ingredients together in a separate bowl. Whisk well.

Remove boiling milk from heat. Immediately add egg mixture and blend. If not thickened well, return to low heat and stir until thickened. Serve cold or warm. Makes a delicious topping for cake with fruit.

—TIMBERLINGS B & B, PALMER

MICROWAVE FRUIT COMPOTE

Apples, pears and pineapple in
  amount needed

1/4 C. brown sugar

1 t. cinnamon

2 T. butter

liqueur to taste

Slice fruit. Mix sugar, cinnamon, butter and liqueur. Pour over fruit in baking pan. Microwave 7 to 8 minutes. Serve warm or refrigerate.

—ARCTIC TERN B & B,
SOLDOTNA

LAYERED BERRY DESSERT

Nut crust layer:

1 C. flour

1/2 C. margarine

1 C. chopped nuts

White layer:

8 oz. cream cheese, room
  temperature

1 C. powdered sugar

8 oz. prepared whipped topping

Berry layer:

1 C. sugar

3 T. cornstarch

1 C. water

3 T. raspberry Jello powder

1 qt. blueberries

Nut Crust: Mix flour and margarine to the consistency of cornmeal; add nuts. Press into 1 9- x 13-inch pan or 2 9-inch round pans. Bake at 350 degrees for 10 minutes. Chill.

White layer: Beat cream cheese and sugar until smooth. Mix in whipped topping. Spread on crust and refrigerate.

Berry layer: Blend sugar and cornstarch; add water. Cook until thick and clear. Add Jello powder and stir until dissolved. Add blueberries to mixture and stir gently to coat berries. Spread on white layer. Chill.

—TUTKA BAY LODGE,
HOMER

PISTACHIO DELIGHT

Crust:

1 C. flour

1/2 C. margarine

2 T. sugar

1/2 C. nuts, chopped

Filling:

1 C. powdered sugar

1 C. Cool Whip

8 oz. cream cheese

Topping:

2 pkg. pistachio instant pudding

2 C. cold milk

1 can crushed pineapple, drained

Cool Whip

chopped nuts

Crust: Mix crust ingredients and press into a 9- x 13-inch pan; bake at 300 degrees until light brown.

Filling: Blend ingredients and spread over crust.

Topping: Combine pudding mix, milk and pineapple. Mix thoroughly and spread over filling. Top with Cool Whip and nuts. Refrigerate.

Variation: Omit pineapple and use chocolate instant pudding.

—MEYERS CHUCK LODGE, MEYERS CHUCK

PEACH COBBLER

1 cup self-rising flour

1 C. sugar

2/3 C. milk

1/2 C. butter

2 large cans peaches

Melt butter in 10- x 15-inch baking dish. Mix flour, sugar and milk in bowl; add melted butter. Do not mix. Place fruit in baking dish; pour batter over, making sure fruit is covered. Bake at 375 degrees until done.

—ARCTIC TERN B & B, SOLDOTNA

PRALINE POWDER DESSERT TOPPING

1 C. whole blanched almonds or
   unblanched hazelnuts, lightly
   toasted

3/4 C. sugar

3 T. light corn syrup

3 T. water

1/4 t. salt, optional

Lightly butter a cookie sheet. Spread the nuts on it and place in a 250-degree oven to warm. Leave them for 10 minutes, shaking the pan once or twice. Turn off the oven, open the oven door, leaving the pan inside.

Combine the sugar, corn syrup, and water in a small heavy saucepan. Bring the mixture to a boil over high heat; after boiling begins, use a wet pastry brush to wipe down any sugar crystals on the sides of the pan. Boil the syrup until it begins to turn a light caramel color—if you use a candy/jelly thermometer, the reading will be between 320 degrees and 340 degrees. Quickly add the salt, if you are using it, and the warmed nuts. Stir the mixture quickly, then pour it onto the buttered cookie sheet that held the nuts; spread it out with a wooden spoon or spatula.

Cool the brittle completely, then break it into small pieces. Working in batches, grind it to a fairly fine powder in a food processor or a blender. Store praline powder in an airtight container. Makes 2 cups. Can be sprinkled onto ice cream, over French toast, or folded into whipped cream for a cake filling.

—RIVERSONG LODGE,
YENTNA RIVER

WILD BLUEBERRY LEMON TART

Shell:

1 1/3 C. all purpose flour

1/4 C. sugar

1/4 t. salt

1/2 C. cold unsalted butter, cut
    into bits

1 large egg yolk, beaten with
    2 T. ice water

2 T. fine lemon zest

Filling:

1 C. buttermilk

3 large egg yolks

1/2 C. sugar

1 T. fine lemon zest, freshly
    grated

1 T. fresh lemon juice

1/4 C. unsalted butter, melted
    and cooled

1 t. vanilla

1/2 t. salt

2 T. all purpose flour

2 C. freshly picked wild
    blueberries, stems removed

confectioner's sugar (garnish)

Shell: Combine flour, sugar and salt, add butter and blend until mixture resembles coarse meal. Add egg yolk mixture and lemon zest; toss until incorporated and form into a ball. Wrap in wax paper and chill for 1 hour. Roll dough out 1/8-inch thick on floured surface. Fit into tart pan with removable bottom and chill at least 30 minutes. Line shell with foil, fill with pie weights or dried beans and bake at 350 degrees for 25 minutes. Remove foil and weights and continue baking 5 to 10 minutes; cool.

Filling: Blend buttermilk, yolks, sugar, zest, lemon juice, butter, vanilla and salt. Add the flour, mixing until smooth. Spread berries evenly over the bottom of the shell; pour on the buttermilk mixture. Bake at 350 degrees 30 to 35 minutes, or until the filling is set. Let cool completely on a rack, sprinkle with confectioner's sugar and serve with vanilla or blueberry swirl ice cream.

**—ALASKA RAINBOW LODGE,
KING SALMON**

CREME DE MENTHE BROWNIES

Brownies:

2 squares (2 oz.) unsweetened
    chocolate, melted

1/2 C. butter or margarine

1 C. sugar

2 eggs

1 t. vanilla

3/4 C. flour

Filling:

1/2 C. margarine or butter,
    softened

3 oz. cream cheese

2 1/2 C. powdered sugar

3 T. Creme de Menthe syrup

green food coloring

Frosting:

6 oz. (1 C.) semisweet chocolate
    chips

1/3 C. margarine

Creme de Menthe candies
    (optional garnish)

mint leaves (optional garnish)

Brownies: Grease bottom of 9- x 13-inch pan. In mixer bowl, mix melted chocolate and butter; stir in sugar. Add eggs and vanilla; beat lightly just until combined (don't overbeat or brownies will fall). Stir in flour and spread in pan; bake at 350 degrees for 30 minutes, then cool completely.

Filling: Combine margarine and cream cheese; beat until fluffy. Add powdered sugar, syrup and food coloring; beat until smooth. Spread evenly over cooled brownies.

Frosting: In small saucepan, stir chocolate and margarine constantly over low heat until smooth Remove from heat; cool 15 minutes. Pour frosting evenly over filling. Freeze the completed brownies for at least 1 hour before cutting into 1-inch squares and serving. Garnish with mint leaves or Creme de Menthe candies. Store in refrigerator.

—ILIASKA LODGE,
ILIAMNA LAKE

Appendix:

Lodges, Inns and Bed & Breakfasts

Alaskan Frontier Gardens Bed and Breakfast
1011 E. Tudor Road #160
Anchorage, AK 99503

Alaska Rainbow Lodge
P.O. Box 96
King Salmon, AK 99613

Alaska's 7 Gables Bed and Breakfast
P.O. Box 80488
Fairbanks, AK 99708

All the Comforts of Home
12531 Turk's Turn
Anchorage, AK 99516

Anchor River Bed and Breakfast
P.O. Box 193
Anchor Point, AK 99556

Arctic Loon Bed and Breakfast
P.O. Box 110333
Anchorage, AK 99511

Arctic Tern Bed and Breakfast
P.O. Box 4381
Soldotna, AK 99669

Backwoods Bed and Breakfast
P.O. Box 3063
Homer, AK 99603

Baranof Wilderness Lodge
Box 210011
Auke Bay, AK 99821

Beach House Bed and Breakfast
P.O. Box 2617-AK
Homer, AK 99603

Bear Creek Bed and Breakfast
41855 Bear Creek Dr.
Homer, AK 99603

Beaver Bend Bed and Breakfast
231 Iditarod
Fairbanks, AK 99701

Bentley's Porter House Bed and Breakfast
P.O. Box 529
Bethel, AK 99559

Best of All Bed and Breakfast
P.O. Box 1578
Valdez, AK 99686

Betty's Bed and Breakfast
248 Madcap Lane
Fairbanks, AK 99709

Big Eddy Bed and Breakfast
44995 Peregrine Place
Soldotna, AK 99669

Big Sky Charter and Fish Camp
13120 Saunders Road
Anchorage, AK 99516

Biorka Bed and Breakfast
611 Biorka Street
Sitka, AK 99835

Blueberry Lodge Bed and Breakfast
9436 North Douglas Highway
Juneau, AK 99801

Bluff House Bed and Breakfast
P.O. Box 39194
Ninilchik, AK 99639

Bowey's Bed and Breakfast
2021 First Avenue
Ketchikan, AK 99901

Brass Ring Bed and Breakfast
987 Hillfair Court
Homer, AK 99603

Camai Bed and Breakfast
3838 Westminster Way
Anchorage, AK 99508

The Chalet Bed and Breakfast
4705 Strawberry Road
Kenai, AK 99611

Creek's Edge Bed and Breakfast
Box 2941
Sitka, AK 99835

Daybreak Bed and Breakfast
798 Chena Hills Drive
Fairbanks, AK 99709

Denali West Lodge
P.O. Box 12
Lake Minchumina, AK 99757

Denali Wilderness Lodge
Box 50
Denali Park, AK 99755

Ede Den Bed and Breakfast
Box 870365
Wasilla, AK 99687

Fairbanks Downtown Bed and Breakfast
851 6th Avenue
Fairbanks, AK 99701

Favorite Bay Inn Bed and Breakfast
P.O. Box 101
Angoon, AK 99820

Four Poster Bed and Breakfast
P.O. Box 663
Homer, AK 99603

Francine's Bed and Breakfast
P.O. Box 3630
Homer, AK 99603

Glacier Bay Country Inn Bed and Breakfast
P.O. Box 5
Gustavus, AK 99826

Good Riverbed and Breakfast
P.O. Box 37
Gustavus, AK 99826

Great Alaska Cedar Works Bed and Breakfast
1527-AK Pond Reef Road
Ketchikan, AK 99901

Gustavus Inn Bed and Breakfast
P.O. Box 60
Gustavus, AK 99826

Hatcher Pass Bed and Breakfast
HC 01 Box 6797-D
Palmer, AK 99645

Iliaska Lodge
P.O. Box 228
Iliamna, AK 99606 (summer)
P.O. Box 30
Homer, AK 99603 (winter)

Jewell's By The Sea
P.O. Box 1662
Petersburg, AK 99833

Kachemak Bay Wilderness Lodge
P.O. Box 956
Homer, AK 99603

Kalsin Bay Inn
P.O. Box 1696
Kodiak, AK 99615

Karras Bed and Breakfast
230 Kogwonton Street
Sitka, AK 99835

Kroto Creek Lodge
P.O. Box 520953
Big Lake, AK 99652

The Last Resort Bed and Breakfast
P.O. Box 1578
Valdez, AK 99686

The Lilac House Bed and Breakfast
950 D Street
Anchorage, AK 99501

Lion's Den Wilderness Lodge
P.O. Box 66
Port Lions, AK 99550

Lisianski Lodge
P.O. Box 776
Pelican, AK 99832

The Lost Chord Bed and Breakfast
2200 Fritz Cove Road
Juneau, AK 99801

Lost Creek Ranch
P.O. Box 84334
Fairbanks, AK 99708

Magic Canyon Ranch Bed and Breakfast
40015 Waterman Road
Homer, AK 99603

Marlow's Kenai River Bed and Breakfast
Box 2465
Soldotna, AK 99669

McCarthy Wilderness Bed and Breakfast
P.O. Box 111241
Anchorage, AK 99511

McKinley/Denali Cabins and Breakfast
Box 90 A
Denali Park, AK 99755

Meyers Chuck Lodge
Meyers Chuck, AK 99903 (summer)
P.O. Box 6141
Ketchikan, AK 99901 (winter)

Northwoods Lodge
P.O. Box 770722
Eagle River, AK 99577

Pacifica Guest House
P.O. Box 1208
Bethel, AK 99559

Pat's Place Bed and Breakfast
Box 870276
Wasilla, AK 99687

Pearson's Pond Bed and Breakfast
4541 Sawa Circle
Juneau, AK 99801

Pollen's Bed and Breakfast
HC01 Box 6005 D
Palmer, AK 99645

Puffin's Bed and Breakfast
P.O. Box 3
Gustavus, AK 99826

Quiet Place Lodge Bed and Breakfast
P.O. Box 6474
Halibut Cove, AK 99603

Redoubt View Bed and Breakfast
Box 4173
Soldotna, AK 99669

Riversong Lodge
2463 Cottonwood St.
Anchorage, AK 99508

Russell's Bed and Breakfast
HC01 Box 6229-R
Palmer, AK 99645

Seldovia Rowing Club Inn Bed
and Breakfast
Box 41
Seldovia, AK 99663

Spruce Acres Bed and Breakfast
Cabins
910 Sterling Highway
Homer, Alaska 99603

The Summer Inn Bed and
Breakfast
P.O. Box 1198
Haines, AK 99827

Sunrise Bed and Breakfast
P.O. Box 632
Sterling, AK 99672

Talbott's Bed and Breakfast
Box 857
Delta Junction, AK 99737

Tern Inn on the Lake Bed and
Breakfast
P.O. Box 1105
Palmer, AK 99645

Timberlings Bed and Breakfast
P.O. Box 732
Palmer, AK 99645

Tolovana Lodge
P.O. Box 281
Nenana, AK 99760

Tutka Bay Lodge
Box 960
Homer, AK 99603

Village Strip Bed and Breakfast
Box 140
Talkeetna, AK 99676

Wallin's Hilltop Bed and Breakfast
P.O. Box 8
Anchor Point, AK 99556

Wasilla Lake Bed and Breakfast
961 North Shore Dr.
Wasilla, AK 99687

Whispering Pond Bed and
Breakfast
Box 3128
Soldotna, AK 99669

Wilson's Hostel Bed and Breakfast
P.O. Box 969
Bethel, AK 99555

Windsock Inn Bed and Breakfast
P. O. Box 240223
Douglas, AK 99824-0223

W.T. Fugarwe Lodge
P.O. Box 280
Gustavus, AK 99826

Wright's Bed and Breakfast
1411 Oxford Drive
Anchorage, AK 99503

Recipe Index